groomgroove.com

presents

DON'T SCREW UP
Your Bride's Wedding

A GROOM'S GUIDE TO SURVIVING THE MOST IMPORTANT DAY OF YOUR WIFE'S LIFE

Michael Arnot
Founder of GroomGroove.com

Adams media
Avon, Massachusetts

GroomGroove is a trademark
of Groove Media LLC.

Published by
Adams Media, an F+W Media Company
57 Littlefield Street, Avon, MA 02322. U.S.A.
www.adamsmedia.com

ISBN 10: 1-59869-597-5
ISBN 13: 978-1-59869-597-7

Printed in Canada.

J I H G F E D C B A

Library of Congress Cataloging-in-Publication Data
is available from the publisher.

This publication is designed to provide accurate and authoritative information with regard to the subject matter covered. It is sold with the understanding that the publisher is not engaged in rendering legal, accounting, or other professional advice. If legal advice or other expert assistance is required, the services of a competent professional person should be sought.
—From a *Declaration of Principles* jointly adopted by a Committee of the American Bar Association and a Committee of Publishers and Associations

Many of the designations used by manufacturers and sellers to distinguish their product are claimed as trademarks. Where those designations appear in this book and Adams Media was aware of a trademark claim, the designations have been printed with initial capital letters.

This book is available at quantity discounts for bulk purchases. For information, please call 1-800-289-0963.

For Nada, my wife, who tried hard to get me to be a smart groom a couple of years ago.

I wasn't a great groom but I'm trying to be a great husband!

Contents

one

Gut Check—Are We Ready to Get Married? 1

two

Popping the Question 13

three

"Man, What Have I Started?"
Early Planning after "YES!" 33

four

Pre-Game Prep 49

five

What Does a Groom Have to Do? 59

six

Picking Your Team: The Best Man and Groomsmen 69

seven

Wedding Wheels, Hired Paparazzi, and Cool Tunes 81

eight

Looking Smart on Wedding Day 97

nine

The Honeymoon: Your Post-Wedding Getaway 107

ten

A Bachelor Party Roadmap 121

eleven

Practice Makes Perfect: Toasts, Speeches, the Rehearsal, and the Rehearsal Dinner 133

twelve

Wedding Week (and More Gifts to Buy) 143

thirteen
Overcoming Last-Minute Jitters 157

fourteen
The Happily-Ever-After Part 165

Introduction

THIS BOOK COMES because of the success of GroomGroove.com, the web's leading engagement and wedding guide for men. I conceived of the idea for GroomGroove.com when I got married. And just so you know, despite the bumps that every couple endures as what seems to be a requirement of marriage, I've been happily married now for several awesome years. However, at the time of my wedding, there were no useful resources for grooms, and certainly none that a man could actually identify with. That's where the idea for GroomGroove.com came from.

I wasn't involved in the wedding planning for my wedding, at all. Admittedly, I cut some bows that my fiancée used for wedding invitations, planned the honeymoon, and sent out thank-you cards. But I barely prepared my wedding speech. And I wasn't terribly interested in scanning gifts with a scanner gun on a Saturday afternoon to add to our gift registry. I did go to a marriage preparation class. (That was very useful and I recommend it heartily.)

All in all, I was just like you—more interested in the sports on TV or a round of golf, or anything else, really, but *The Big Day*. Now the truth is, I would have gotten my marriage started on a much better footing if I just *seemed* like I was pumped to participate in the wedding, rather than along for the ride. And so, even if you're more or less enthused than I was, you'll earn a ton of bonus points just by doing those things that are on your list of things to do, and maybe even biting off a little more. It really doesn't have to be more complicated than that. And who knows—you might just find that you have a knack for tying bows or planning honeymoon activities!

This book wouldn't be possible without the hardworking people at GroomGroove.com. First and foremost, Aubree Wyatt Smith, our creative director, who has a keen eye for what's hot in weddings, and what guys actually care about. Brett Meyer, our Web developer (who, at the time of writing, had just popped the question); Ralph Arend, our videographer; Matthew Arnot, one of our writers (and my brother); and Nick Stamoulis of Brick Marketing round out our team. We've been fortunate to have on board numerous contributors, and fans. We also happen to think that grooms, the best men, and groomsmen of the world visiting our site and coming back frequently are also a big part of it. And now, they have this book!

A Letter to the Bride
from the Guys
at GroomGroove.com

IF YOU ARE THE BRIDE— READ THIS FIRST!

Dear Bride-to-be . . .

Surprise! This book is not for you; it's for your fiancé. For once, here's something useful written for him on the subject of weddings. You may not know it right now, but in your hand is a little wedding savior, which means you should buy it for him, fast!

Now, it's your "Big Day," and you have visions of roses, lilies, and gerbera daisies adorning every table, chair, and little girl's ear. But the first thing you need to know about men and weddings is that your fiancé doesn't really give a damn about wedding flowers. (Shocking, yes, we know.)

It's not that he doesn't want you to be happy or that he doesn't care about the wedding, it's just that he doesn't care . . . about flowers. And if he took as much of an interest in flowers as you, then we hope for your sake he's a florist. (Wouldn't *that* be convenient.)

The second thing you need to know is that weddings are not just a "sport" for women. To use a sports analogy your fiancé will understand, when it comes to your wedding, you're the coach of the team. With the right coaching, your fiancé can and will "give 110 percent" to make the wedding of your dreams go off without a hitch. Buy this book for him and send him to GroomGroove.com. Tell him he's doing a great job by reading up on the things that he can do in preparation for your impending nuptials, and—reading between the lines—in preparation for marriage. That's a real sign of his desire to get involved. Flowers? Not so much.

Sincerely,
The Guys at GroomGroove.com

A Letter to the Groom
from the Guys
at GroomGroove.com

IF YOU ARE THE GROOM—READ THIS FIRST!

Dear Groom-to-be . . .

Congratulations, and all that jazz. Getting married is a rite of passage akin to a rookie initiation for a sports team, but with more flowers and dresses. The coach of this team is your fiancée. She has sized you up, and, frankly, she's hoping you'll put in a 50 percent effort and not be a weak link. But you, the eager-to-impress rookie—well—you're going to give 110 percent.

We know that most of the wedding section of the bookstore is filled with frilly, pink books written for women. It is, after all, your glorious fiancée (memorize those two words, by the way) who is going to choose the flowers and plan most of the event. Remember, she may very well have been assembling a wedding fantasy in her mind since she was a little girl.

That said, from bachelor to husband, you're about to undergo a transformation. You have taken the initiative by buying this book (or by having it thrust into your arms like a football in the hands of a running back). In any event, the purpose of this book is to help you in areas where men struggle to stay awake, stay interested, and add value: the wedding-planning process.

But now, it's game time.

In this playbook, we're going to cover everything from whether you are really ready to get married to popping the question and arranging the bachelor party, wedding transportation, wedding ceremony, and honeymoon. Weeks from now, you will suddenly find yourself uttering words and phrases you didn't even know that you knew—and didn't know—until now. Just by flipping through this book, you're going to be rookie of the year, without really even trying.

Finally, let's break the huddle, and offer you congratulations on finding "The One." Best wishes for your wedding, and more importantly, for your marriage.

Sincerely,
The Guys at GroomGroove.com

one

Gut Check—Are We Ready to Get Married?

THOUGHT WE'D JUMP right to diamond engagement rings and popping the question, did you? Or the difference between cut, color, clarity, and carat size? Or distinctions between a Las Vegas or Montreal bachelor party? Not quite yet. We're going to take this nice and slow.

This first chapter will help you figure out whether you should keep reading this book or just return it to the bookstore. And not because you don't like the book ... but perhaps because you didn't like the answers to the questions you're going to ask of yourself about getting married. Don't be scared. You'll thank us for making you think. Communication allows you to cut through the nonsense to make sure you're really ready to get married and is the basis for building a great marriage.

HOW DO I KNOW SHE'S "THE ONE"?

How do I know she's "The One"? It's the ultimate question asked by billions of men before you and will be asked by billions after. Of course, if you've asked any of your buddies, they'll have already given you that oh-so-unhelpful answer: "I guess I just knew . . . ."

Without wanting to toss in the towel too quickly, there is an element of truth to the idea that you'll just *know* that your current girlfriend is destined to be your retirement partner in Florida. *Knowing* is that feeling you get when you've got the right combination of characteristics in, first, the woman and, second, the relationship itself. The fact that you've got this book in your hands is a good indicator that you're onto something. Unless, of course, it was a gift. From your girlfriend. As a hint. Read on.

The Woman

What is it about this particular woman that makes you want to commit to her as a life partner? Contrary to what your mother would have you believe, only you can define the characteristics you're looking for. What is it about this woman (over and above the others that have already danced around in your life and possibly dumped you) that makes your heart jump? Is she smart,

2

sporty, and funny? Is she ballsy? Is it her looks? Is it *only* her looks? Is there anyone in the world you'd rather be with?

The Golf Driving Range Test

We suggest spending quality time alone thinking about why your girlfriend is the woman you should marry. What better way to reflect than by hitting golf balls at the driving range? (This won't be the last time that sports and weddings intersect—think of the honeymoon!) Hit a bucket of balls, and, say for every third ball or so, build a checklist in your head. The point is not to improve your five iron (though that may be an added benefit), but to really analyze how you feel about your girlfriend and whether you are ready to commit to her and the "institution of marriage." Now, if you want a real challenge (or golf isn't your thing), get a pen and paper and spend thirty minutes writing down the reasons why she's the one you want. We'd bet you haven't done this kind of thinking in any serious way. And that's okay, because this kind of deep reflection doesn't always yield a grocery list of identifiable reasons to marry your girlfriend. Nor, for that matter, will it always yield easily digestible and happy results. That said, it's a valuable exercise. When you're done with your list, you're either going to have:

- A piece of paper that your fiancée will later use to write her actual grocery list on, only to pause at the store when she notices one of the items is "She's pretty nice."

  Or

- A nice little list of things to say to your bride just before you utter those immortal words: "Will you marry me?"

A RELATIONSHIP WORTH A LIFETIME

So how are you going to know whether you've got a relationship worthy of committing to for a lifetime? What are some of the characteristics that'll make or break your marriage? Hopefully, your relationship features good communication, cooperation, and understanding.

Open Communication and Conflict-Resolution Strategies

If you've got shared goals and desires (including support for respective careers, views on having a family, and a sense of life trajectory), you have the key elements of a successful marriage and you will be in good stead. If you enjoy being with your girlfriend and she enjoys being with you, but you're both secure enough to have lives outside of the relationship, you've got something to hang on to. If you're not just dependent on each other but inter-dependent, that's a good sign.

Communication. Yeah, we know it's a bit of a cliché and a big statement, but come your next big blowup, you'll know whether you have open communication and conflict-resolution strategies. And if you really don't have any arguments, do you know if you've got a way to de-escalate conflict? If you're figuring out now that you don't have an approach to cool things down when arguments get heated, that's not a deal-breaker but rather a sign that you've got work to do with your wife-to-be.

Compromise from time to time. Yes, even you. The little compromises will mean a lot to both of you, and you've got to be willing to bend a little if your relationship is going to last a lifetime. Compromise means doing things you'd rather not be doing, like reading an awesome book about weddings for guys. We hear you. It also means figuring out to what extent your views of your life trajectories match up. Read on.

Selflessness, rather than selfishness. Selfishness in any relationship, let alone your marriage, is a recipe for disaster and a major turnoff. Selfishness is at the root of all future marital problems.

Mutual respect. The woman you are marrying is not a trophy. You have got to respect her for her intelligence, kindness, and caring.

We at GroomGroove.com believe that you can get everything in life that you want, if you'll only just help your wife get everything in life that she wants. Make that your mantra, and you'll have a relationship with which to build a successful marriage.

Now, it's possible that you'll not be able to check all of these off. You may bottle up all of your feelings ("I'm a man, I don't have feelings . . .") and your relationship may not feature great communication or conflict-resolution strategies. Your girlfriend is not likely to be perfect, and if you're searching for perfection, you'll be doing that for a long and probably lonely lifetime.

SURE, IT'S A WEDDING, BUT IT'S ALSO A MARRIAGE

Okay. So your girlfriend is definitely (or at least, in some definitive way) "The One." The next step in preventing a visit to your local divorce lawyer in three years is to figure out if the collective "you" is really ready to be married. That is, are you both *really* ready to get married?

Below are Ten Tough Questions (what we at GroomGroove.com call a "Gut Check") which basically amount to a series of discussions that you need to have with your girlfriend before you take the plunge. Indeed, this gut check will help prevent you from cracking your head on the bottom of the pool, so to speak. (It happens.)

Ten Tough Questions

The Ten Tough Questions are really categories of discussion points to foster an open and frank dialogue with your girlfriend about what might be unspoken expectations and relationship issues that could exist or develop between the two of you. If you're really smart, you'll sit down with your girlfriend, book in hand, and knock these questions out of the ballpark, one by one.

1. "Are we having children?" Are we ever having children? Are we, or are either one of us, going to take time away from our respective careers to be the primary caregiver? Who is going to pick up our kids from day care? How many children do we want to have? Are we willing to plan for the next eighteen years of our lives? Do we both believe that marriage means children? Can we afford children? Is having a child more about filling a gap in our dark little souls? When would we have children? What have we learned from our parents? Am I ready to be a dad? Are you ready to be a mom?

2. "I don't want to talk about it." Have we developed proper means of resolving conflict and general communication? Do we shelve issues to deal with "later?" If communications break down, are we both willing to take steps toward improving them, including professional help?

3. "Till death do us part . . ." Do we really enjoy spending time together, or have we just become mutually dependent? Are we really in love, for the long run? Are we just settling for the sake of convenience? Are we going to spend time with each other's friends? Do we even like each other's friends? Are they a good influence on us? Are we committed to making this work, through thick and thin, sickness and health, for richer or for poorer, for the long haul, till death do us part? Or will we be inclined to abandon our commitment when difficulties arise?

4. "I got a job offer . . . in Dubai." How focused are we on our careers or profession? Do we understand each other's professional expectations? How ambitious are we? Who has the more flexible job? If one of us gets a promotion and needs to relocate, how will we decide what to do? Can we handle the strain of long workdays or extended travel?

5. "I can't stand your mom." Are there issues with each other's family? Are there competing family traditions in areas of work ethic, lifestyle, or general expectations that might make marriage difficult? How can we accommodate our different backgrounds in one household? How much time do we plan to spend with each other's family? How will we accommodate holidays?

6. "Please stop clipping your toenails in my presence." Are there personal habits that we each find annoying? How can we change these habits without sacrificing our core personalities? Are we each able to bring up these issues without causing a blow out? How will we each have our "me" time away from each other? Does one of us find this more important than the other one does?

7. "Let's have sex ... next month." Is our sex life going to keep us happy for the long term? How often are we likely to want sex? Do we both believe in monogamy? (This is the last person you will ever sleep with, after all.) How can we continue to make sex interesting? How can we make sex a relationship goal and long-term project? Can we talk openly about our sexuality and our desires?

8. "Hey, that's my carton of milk.... " Do we both share fiscal responsibility? (Or are we both equally irresponsible!) Am I a spender, and you a saver? Have we figured out a method for everyday banking? Do we both understand how our financial resources should influence purchases? Are we comfortable with the lifestyle our income will

produce? What are our future income expectations? Do we believe that money buys happiness?
What kind of a budget should we have? What kind
of financial planning makes sense for us? Do we
have massive debt? What kind of banking arrangements should we be making, and when?

**9. "What do you mean, there's more than one
God?"** Do we share the same morals or are there
differences of opinion? Are we planning to raise
our children with a set of core values? What are
the fundamental principles that we both share?
How will we reasonably accommodate different
religious beliefs? How will religion affect our daily
lives and identity within our community? What
role will religion play in our lives?

10. "Dan's hosting poker night. . . ." Are we able
to have friends outside of our marriage? As we'll be
seeing a lot of each other (more than we ever did in
the past), are we comfortable with "night out with
the boys," sports night, or other activities that don't
involve each other's company? Do we have a strategy to ensure that we each maintain our separate
identity, and foster the friendships that we had
before being married?

GUT CHECKED: (WE ARE READY!)

What should follow these inquiries is the proverbial chat with yourself in the mirror. This is when you take the time to go over the answers and weigh the significance of each response. Did you find surprising differences of opinion? Why were any of the answers surprising? Is it time to shave your goatee?

Instead of conveniently ignoring the differences or assuming sacrifices will occur, realize now that these may be reasons that add up to "irreconcilable differences" in the petition for divorce, in the future. Ask yourself, despite those differences, if this is the person who will help you live your happiest, fullest life? Can you promise her the same? Remember that a happy and fulfilled wife means a happy and fulfilled life. We guess that only you'll know the answer. If the answer is yes, and we hope so, then congratulations! If the answer is no, that's okay too. Better to have figured this out now. If the answer is maybe, then you may be on the road to marrying this person, but have to tackle some of the barriers before getting down on one knee. Wherever you're at, be honest with your girlfriend and yourself.

two

Popping the Question

DIAMONDS ARE SUPPOSED to be forever, and you should be thinking about this slogan as you are preparing for the proposal. The ring you choose will (or should, at least) stay with your bride for the rest of her life, so take your time, do some research, and (these days) maybe even go shopping with your fiancée.

BUYING THE BLING-BLING

The next step after concluding that you're ready to skip down the path to marriage is to figure out the details of an engagement ring and marriage proposal. To be a smart groom, you'll need to learn a little bit about engagement rings before making a purchase and executing a proposal.

Selecting the Ring of Choice

You're not likely to know your girlfriend's bra size, let alone ring size. While a bra size is infinitely more important than ring size, forget *Victoria's Secret* for now and get to know your girl's ring finger.

> ### TIPS FOR THE SMART GROOM
>
> Your girlfriend's bra size is indicated on the tag of one of her bras. (Who knew?) GroomGroove.com features a lingerie-buying guide for grooms that we suggest you visit. Presents during your engagement (any time, really) are sure to make her happy!

Fortunately, there is an easy solution to figuring out your girlfriend's ring size, and it doesn't involve any numbers. If she owns any rings, she may take them off from time to time. You should play James Bond one evening and sneak the ring away to the bathroom or kitchen. There, you can make an impression of the ring in a bar of soap or potato. Take it to the jeweler, and you've hit a home run. If you make a mistake, that's generally not a problem, as rings can be resized.

While it's said that the size of the rock does matter to many women, the style of the engagement ring is far more important. Does she prefer platinum, yellow, or white gold? Does she prefer simple styles, or would she prefer an engagement ring that will be instantly noticed? Diamonds, or some other gemstone? By studying the kind of jewelry she typically wears and paying close attention to the hints she will inevitably drop, you can deduce valuable bits of information. Your goal is to buy a ring that reflects her personality.

TIPS FOR THE SMART GROOM

The smart groom can lead his fiancée to the local jewelry store "by accident." "Let's go in to look at some seriously hideous jewelry," you could say. (Jewelry stores are often chockfull of incredible pieces that only a teenage girl or loving grandmother would wear!) Be attentive to any jewelry that she admires. Or navigate to an online jewelry store. Find the ugliest rings you can find, and show them to her to throw her off the scent. Then you can quietly navigate to an area of the site where she'll pick out the rings that really appeal to her.

LEARN ALL ABOUT DIAMONDS

Learn about diamonds and the four "Cs": clarity, cut, color, and carat. Don't know what those words mean yet? That's okay. What follows below is really only an introduction. But make sure to do your own research before visiting the jeweler.

The Four "Cs"—Finding That Perfect Stone

Cut (What's the Shape of the Rock?)

It takes a skilled artisan to cut a diamond into its ideal shape. The cut refers to the shape of the whole diamond, rather than just the face of the diamond. A diamond cutter's goal is to maximize brilliance and sparkle. The more experienced the craftsperson, the better the result working with the raw material; the results are independently graded by organizations such as the Gemological Institute of America (GIA). A diamond that is cut too deep or too shallow will fail to shine as brightly and may appear dull.

> ### TIPS FOR THE SMART GROOM
>
> If your bride is likely to want to show off a massive rock, purchase a diamond that is a shade on the shallow side. It'll appear larger. Ask your jeweler to see stones that are cut this way and do not sacrifice the *bling* factor. You may not find something as we've described, but it's worth a shot.

Cut also refers to the shape of the face of the diamond. Round is the most common shape, but you can also choose from shapes such as princess, emerald, oval, pear, and heart. The right shape is based entirely on your fiancée's preferences.

If she's never mentioned which shape she finds most appealing, stick with a round or princess cut. Round cuts are easily the most popular choice.

Color (Is This Rock Clear or Does It Have a Pee-in-the-Snow Tinge to It?)

Diamonds are graded on a color scale ranging from D (colorless) to Z (yellowish). The closer you get to the D rating, the more expensive (and presumably more appealing) the diamond will be. That said, many brides prefer jewelry that isn't colorless, and most antique jewelry comes this way. Color is particularly important if the color itself can be seen by the naked eye. You may not be able to notice any difference between a D, E, or F, but you may start to see yellowness at J. Color tends to affect the price significantly.

D–F: Colorless
G–J: Almost colorless
K–M: Faint yellow
N–R: Pale yellow
S–Z: Light yellow

*Note: These ratings are set under controlled lighting conditions, and very well may be indistinguishable in the real world. If your purchase decision comes down to, say, a J- and an I-rated diamond, and you can't tell any difference between the two, go with the more economical rating.

Clarity (Is the Diamond a Bit Cloudy, and If So, Why?)

Almost all diamonds have imperfections. Flaws, such as mineral deposits or fractures, are called inclusions. The more inclusions in a diamond, the less brilliantly it will shine. Inclusions can be tough to spot with the naked eye, but if the overall look of a diamond is cloudy or dull despite cleaning, then you know you've got a diamond with a lot of inclusions.

You should ask to look at the diamond through a loupe (and have your jeweler show you how to use the loupe) and a light as part of your diamond shopping. You may be surprised at what you find. Just keep in mind that virtually all diamonds out there have imperfections—if you can't see it with the naked eye, it's not a deal-breaker for that particular stone.

Clarity is ranked on how visible the flaws are at a magnification of 10×. The clarity scale ranges from F (flawless) to I (included).

F: No inclusions.
VVS1–VVS2: Minute flaws barely visible with magnification.
VS1–VS2: Some minor inclusions seen with magnification.
SI1–SI2: Inclusions noticeable only with magnification.
I1–I3: Some flaws are visible to the naked eye.

Some inclusions at the base of the diamond can be hidden with the mounting. Once mounted, you'll have a diamond that appears to be perfect, despite some imperfections.

Carat (How Big Is the Rock?)

The carat is actually the diamond's measure of weight. One carat measures 200 milligrams. While related to size, cut and mounting also contribute to making a diamond appear to be larger or smaller, so don't look to carat size alone when determining the difference in size between two diamonds.

In fact, when combined with a wedding band that has diamonds in a channel setting, you might be able to achieve a significant amount of sparkle, even if the main stone is less than one carat. Furthermore, if the engagement ring has a center stone but is surrounded by two diamonds on each side, you'll have maximized the sparkle, without increasing the price dramatically.

Men and Engagement Rings

If you don't feel competent enough to buy an engagement ring by yourself, enlist the help of one of your girlfriend's friends or her mother(!). However, be aware that more and more women prefer to choose their own engagement jewelry. This may mean proposing without a ring or with a picture of a ring. Your girlfriend may prefer to be part of the ring selection process rather than be stuck with a ring she finds god-awful. As long as you buy the ring within a month after your proposal, it is perfectly acceptable to propose without it. Obviously, this is less romantic, less fun, and less risky. Nevertheless, it is an acceptable option.

TIPS FOR THE SMART GROOM

One carat is often a "magic number" for diamonds. Because of this, there may be a bit of a price jump from .99 carat to one carat. Craftspeople are often chastised for ending up with a .99 carat diamond when a one carat could have been achieved. Their mistake is your gain—grab the .99 carat diamond ring for a price break and an indiscernible difference. Here's to rounding up.

Other Styles

Your bride may not want an engagement ring that looks like everybody else's. It's very important that you seek the advice of your girlfriend, either directly or covertly, to see if there's a particular ring style that she really likes or can't stand. However, you should know that you're entering dangerous territory if you purchase a custom-designed ring or a ring that is particularly different from the norm. You can cross your fingers that she'll love whatever you buy, but if she likes alternative styles, get out a lollipop ring and visit her favorite jeweler later!

PLATINUM, WHITE GOLD, AND YELLOW GOLD

As if you didn't have enough to learn when it came to the diamond engagement ring, now we're going to cover the question of which metal is the right choice for your ring. When it comes to the diamond engagement ring, you're limited to platinum, "yellow" gold, and "white" gold.

Platinum

Platinum is the king of the precious metals. It's exceedingly rare and quite hefty. According to the Platinum Guild International, an industry group, all the platinum in the world would only fill an Olympic swimming pool to *ankle* deep. Furthermore, a six-inch cube of platinum weighs in at about 165 pounds. Platinum offers a gunmetal sheen that isn't likely to lose its luster over time. That said, platinum is a commodity, and therefore its price fluctuates. However, no matter the price it will always be more expensive than elemental gold or yellow gold. Platinum is measured by purity, like gold. Instead of karats, however, platinum is measured in points or percentages. A typical platinum ring will contain 90 or 95 percent pure platinum, and some other alloy. Chemistry, anyone?

Yellow Gold

Yellow gold is gold in its elemental form, with an alloy that doesn't change the elemental gold's color. Yellow gold is the most traditional engagement ring metal, and 18 karat gold is the most common purity. 18 karat gold represents a ring that is around 75 percent elemental gold, and 25 percent alloyed. Twenty-four karat gold, or pure gold, is never used for jewelry as it is too soft for everyday use. Fourteen karat gold is next on the list, but this represents only about 52 percent elemental gold. The flip-side is that the 14 karat gold ring will not scratch as easily. Yellow gold has become less popular in recent years, as white gold or platinum engagement rings tend to better show off the diamond they are transporting than yellow gold. Nevertheless, yellow gold remains a personal preference for many women.

White Gold

White gold is an increasingly popular choice for engagement rings, as it is a less expensive metal than platinum, but is different from a yellow gold ring. Make no mistake, however; white gold is gold in its elemental form alloyed with some other metal to give it a silvery sheen. White gold is often alloyed with palladium or silver. The only real drawback to white gold is that over time it will tend to show its yellow roots. They can be replated, however. Many women believe that white gold will better show off their diamond engagement ring, and they are probably right.

TWO MONTHS' SALARY ("TWO?!")

Once you have decided on a ring style, it's time to figure out how much you can spend on the biggest piece of jewelry you're ever going to buy. Traditionally, a man is expected to spend at least the equivalent of two months' salary. As we'll discuss below, we don't buy into the two months' salary calculation. The industry has high barriers for purchasing, and your fiancée has high expectations for her fantasy wedding. There are several traditional and practical reasons why the engagement ring is expected to be so costly:

- To demonstrate that you have made the conscious effort of saving money.
- To reiterate that you can support her through difficult and trying times.
- To ensure that, should you and your wife ever find yourselves in financial ruins, there will always be the ring to pawn.

Fortunately, times have changed, and spending a lesser amount is acceptable in the twenty-first century. The pressure to "prove your worth" by spending two months' salary has been relaxed, especially with the advent of online jewelry retailers and retailers offering massive discounts. However, you're likely to spend at least $2,500 on a diamond engagement ring, and probably more than that. A $2,500 diamond engagement ring will have a very nice diamond or several smaller diamonds but will sacrifice one of the four Cs: cut, clarity, color, or carat size of the diamond or be a combination of smaller, less expensive diamonds. Your jeweler can assist you in finding the right combination of the four Cs. You're looking for the right balance of quality and price. If you're on a budget, the best place to buy will be a store with large purchasing power—that means Costco, Zales, or another large retailer. Furthermore, these stores will have a selection of alternatives, such as engagement rings that sport several smaller diamonds.

WHERE TO BUY

There are really two places where you can buy a diamond engagement ring: at a traditional jewelry store or online. Before you stroll confidently into a jewelry store or large chain store, stop for a moment and remember that this is the most important piece of jewelry you'll ever buy. Find out about the jewelers in your area. You will want to do some phone research. Who sells the highest quality of stones for the best value? You will also want to consider the jewelers' policies on warranties and service. If you're buying a diamond-set ring, you and your fiancée may want some assurance that the stone is a conflict-free diamond engagement ring. You'll also want resizing included in the price and a guarantee for a certain period against the loss of the stone due to faulty craftsmanship or defects in the materials used.

TIPS FOR THE SMART GROOM

If you or your wife do not bring in the diamond engagement ring for a cleaning and inspection every six months, you may void the warranty on your store-bought diamond engagement ring. It's not an unreasonable policy, and it is a very good idea to have the prongs holding the diamond in place inspected.

The In-Store 10 Percent Strategy

Be a smart and confident groom (and diamond shopper). It's a bit like approaching your girlfriend and now fiancée the first time. Confidence allowed you to "get the girl." Guys are just as clueless with women as they are with diamonds—so we fake it. Get reasonably smart on diamonds, and throw in some fake confidence in your knowledge. Combine this with a tested strategy for price negotiation as follows. Decide on two or three shops, give them your maximum budget, minus 10 percent, and ask to see the available collections. Why minus 10 percent? Often, jewelers try to tempt you into spending more than you can afford. If you tell them what your real budget is, they will almost invariably show you a few pieces that are slightly above your maximum budget. You can play the jewelers' game by giving them a fake "maximum budget." By telling them a number that is 10 percent less than what you are really prepared to spend, you'll be more likely to stay within your real budget.

Make sure the metal is properly hallmarked, that the diamonds carry a GIA certificate including the carat and grading of the stone, and that the jeweler provides a guarantee that the diamonds are conflict-free. Once you've bought your chosen engagement ring, all that remains is for you to find the perfect moment to put the rock on display.

Buying an Engagement Ring Online

You may have bought music at iTunes or a book at Amazon.com. Increasingly, you may be pointing and clicking to buy your girlfriend's engagement ring. Now, a book and music is one thing, but a diamond engagement ring is something else. With the advent of online ring shopping comes the weighty question of consumer confidence. With so much at stake, it can be difficult for a groom to fork over several thousand dollars on a diamond engagement ring when he can't actually observe for the four Cs.

TIPS FOR THE SMART GROOM

The Gemological Institute of America (GIA) and its competitor organizations are nonprofits that independently grade diamonds. By means of a certified report, the purchaser of a diamond engagement ring can know the precise details of the diamond engagement ring that he has purchased. In fact, the GIA invented the concept of the four Cs, and each of those is listed in precise detail on the report. While some rings do not automatically come with a GIA report, any diamond can be graded by the GIA for a small fee. If you're buying a traditional round cut, single stone diamond engagement ring, ask that the stone be rated by the GIA.

You'll want to do some research, read reviews, and make sure the company's website is secure for making credit card purchases. Major sites like BlueNile.com and Ice.com offer excellent deals and diamond reports from the GIA. If you have this certificate in hand, there really is little chance you can go wrong. Many online retailers expect that you'll have seen a diamond before, up close, and will have an idea of what is the right price-quality rapport. Make sure you're one of those guys.

POPPING THE QUESTION

The ring is sleeping in the ring box and you're ready to pop the question. After this stage, the clock begins to tick toward the wedding day. The proposal is the all-important deal-sealing verbal offer that will commit you to married life. But how are you going to ask her to become Mrs. Right? Given its importance, the prospective groom will want to take some time to think about how to make the marriage proposal memorable. This means you'll want to carefully plan ... something. It could be something elaborate or something simple, but above all, avoid any impulses to propose to your girlfriend spontaneously. You might not feel like a creative person into emotional outpourings of love, but it won't kill you to do it right, just once. That said, an incredible number of couples do just stumble through the marriage proposal by having a conversation on the couch. The guys at Groom-Groove.com implore you to do better.

Regardless of the tone of the proposal or the amount of creativity involved, you do not want your proposal to be overly complicated unless you are prepared for things going wrong. We firmly believe in erring on the side of keeping it simple.

TIPS FOR THE SMART GROOM

It is customary to ask the father of the bride if you may have his daughter's hand in marriage. Now, we said it's customary, but it's also a bit antiquated, formal, and possibly misogynistic. It might make you appear to be more of a gentleman, albeit a gentleman from around 1952. In the twenty-first century, it's your call as to whether you want to do this at all. You may consider asking your girlfriend's father for his blessing rather than for his permission. Furthermore, you could have this conversation with her parents (both father and mother) rather than following last century's rules.

Big Bang or Something Subtle

When you are planning the proposal, you should consider your girlfriend's personality. We hope that you know her well! Is she extroverted or introverted? Does she like being the center of attention? Is she easily impressed? Does she like public displays of affection? We're not asking you to do deep psychological analysis, but you do need to determine whether your girlfriend would appreciate a huge public display or would rather have an intimate moment alone with you. Your proposal should be a reflection more of her personality than of yours.

Where to Do It

Where you actually propose is a very important consideration. It might be where you went on your first date or where you shared some great memories. It could be at a park, a national landmark, a beautiful restaurant, or a foreign locale. You'll want to survey the location to make sure that the idea in your head can be executed on the field. Call ahead. Check the weather. Check the weather even if the proposal is going to be indoors. Your girlfriend probably doesn't want to get engaged on the rainiest day of the year, even if it goes off without a hitch!

WHAT TO SAY WHEN THE TIME COMES

We suggest that you put some words before "Will you marry me?" If you've thought about why you want to spend the rest of your life with your girlfriend and written down in a letter to yourself the reasons why you feel so strongly about this person, you'll have the key points for what you'll want to say when the time comes. Of course, you're not writing a script for a movie. And even if you were, memorize that script!

Making the marriage proposal itself is pretty simple. Get down on one knee, pull out the ring, and tell her why you think she is the greatest person you have ever known and why you love her. All of the preparation, surprise proposal ideas, and creativity you've concocted are fun and games compared to the moment itself.

SURPRISE, SURPRISE, SHE SAID "YES!"

Cue the romantic music. Exit bachelor, stage right. Enter fiancé (that's you) stage left. Welcome to the rest of your life. Now, there's a substantial amount of work to be done from this point forward—are you ready? It'll take you a couple of weeks to transition from calling her "my girlfriend" to "my fiancée," and that'll be a nice little shock the first time it happens.

Most of the time, your fiancée will take the lead on the wedding planning. However, with frequent visits to GroomGroove.com and this book in your hands, you'll be a smart groom and have the opportunity to go beyond what your buddies, your father, and his father did to prepare for their wedding day. The wedding is a rite of passage. It's not the kind of thing to let slide on by, and doing it right builds some serious credibility with your wife-to-be.

WHAT IF SHE SAYS "UMM . . . NO"?

Your girlfriend is not going to say "No." Why are we so sure? That's because you are going to know the answer to the question "Will you marry me?" long before asking the question. In fact, you're not going to ask the question if there's real doubt in your mind as to what she'll say. Pretty easy, isn't it?

three

"Man, What Have I Started?" Early Planning after "YES!"

JUST WHEN YOU thought your job was done, the fun is just getting started. First, congrats on a successful marriage proposal! Now for round two.

Round two begins a couple of days after the engagement when wedding planning starts to pop up into conversations that used to be dominated by where to go for a date on Saturday night. "Where do we want to get married?" your glorious bride-to-be will ask. "And when?"

Yes, it's the infamous "when" and "where" of wedding planning. Did you think that by proposing, you'd put off the question of marriage for a little while? Nope—a marriage proposal puts the pedal to the metal on wedding planning.

As a first step, you may want to announce your wedding to the world (or at least, to your buddies).

TELLING YOUR FAMILY AND FRIENDS

Your newly minted fiancée has likely been on the phone for several hours over the past couple of days letting everyone know that she's engaged. She'll be gushing about the rock, about the marriage proposal, about wedding plans, about dresses and flowers, and so on, and maybe, just maybe, about you as well.

You should soon call your parents and siblings to let them know how it all went (assuming they knew in advance). They'll all be happy for you. You can both expect to be ecstatic at marrying, and she will probably be ecstatic about wedding planning. You and wedding planning? Not so much. That's okay. You're a guy. We hear you.

PUBLIC ANNOUNCEMENT OF THE ENGAGEMENT

Typically printed in your local newspaper or a major newspaper, a public engagement announcement highlights that

- You and your fiancée are getting married,
- Your father-in-law owns a small plastics company in Albuquerque and your mother is a teacher, and so on,

- Both sets of parents are proud of this fact, and
- You both attended wonderful schools and are on the way to successful careers as [insert careers].

We're not entirely convinced of the appropriateness of the abundance of information in engagement announcements about the schools you attended or what your in-laws do for a living. A classy engagement announcement should be as simple as a declaration of your engagement. (That's the point, right?)

The engagement announcement should appear in the newspaper within a couple of months after the engagement and no later than four months before the actual wedding. Chances are your fiancée's parents will suggest and pay for the privilege of gracing the newsprint of your local paper. No matter who pays, it's a nice touch. If no one has taken the step of organizing its publication, why not surprise everyone by taking charge?

Part of the public announcement is the engagement picture. Along with the written section of your engagement notice, a photo can appear in the newspaper as the centerpiece of the announcement. We suggest having engagement photos taken professionally, and most wedding photographers offer this service. (And by the way, there's no pressure on you to hire your engagement photographer as your wedding photographer, although that might be a natural choice.)

Not all newspapers offer to print engagement announcements, but prefer to print only wedding announcements (that is, when it's all done). Either is acceptable.

CHOOSING THE DATE

The most common time of year for weddings is known as "wedding season": the late spring, summer, and early fall. If you're considering a spring or summer wedding, start making reservations approximately ten years prior to even meeting your girlfriend. Photographers, limos, caterers, florists, the band or DJ, and other logistical pieces of the wedding puzzle are going to be booked with other weddings as the date approaches.

Convenience for the Principal Players

The primary attendees needed for the wedding are you, your fiancée, and the wedding party. Therefore, you should consider the timing of the wedding day given your collective work and vacations schedules. Some occupations, such as teachers (and professional athletes, bless them), have a substantial and relaxing off-season during the summer. You and your groomsmen may not. You'll want to avoid holding your wedding during a sacred religious week, on homecoming weekend for your college, or on your grandmother's eighty-fifth birthday. The least expensive period for weddings is during the cold, winter months, but substantial savings can be had by considering a May/June or October/November wedding, just on the fringes of peak wedding season.

WHAT'S YOUR TYPE OF WEDDING?

You can choose from a variety of themes for your wedding. Weddings offer much in the way of flexible costs and styles. For example, you could host any of the following:

An outdoor wedding: a relaxing public venue (weather be damned)

A small wedding: intimate venue, (relatively) inexpensive with fewer than seventy-five guests

A grand wedding: large venue, more expensive with more than 150 guests

A home-style wedding: in your backyard, with buffet-style food service

A destination wedding: a weekend in a special locale, ideally somewhere you and your guests would like to vacation

DESTINATION WEDDINGS

If getting married while on vacation sounds like fun, a destination wedding to a Caribbean locale or Hawaii may be on your radar screen. While weddings themselves are a big undertaking, planning a wedding in Aruba or elsewhere adds an interesting dimension.

A destination wedding will necessarily be a smaller affair. Your guest list will be chipped away as the invitations marked "regrets" pile up, and unfortunately, some of the people who really matter to you may not be able to make it. That said, you might be surprised at the number of friends and family who will jump at the chance to attend a destination wedding.

TIPS FOR THE SMART GROOM

Wouldn't it be great to have an outdoor wedding on a smoking hot July day, complete with a caterer that specializes in barbecue, and bartenders serving up keg after keg of your favorite beer? Doesn't that just seem awesome? It's the kind of wedding reception that guys dream of when they're thinking of their wedding. The guys at GroomGroove.com wish it would happen more often. Hey, there's no harm in suggesting it to your fiancée—but we don't expect good results.

On the logistical front, you're likely to liaise with a wedding planner or with a resort that caters to weddings planned from afar. Ideally, they'll have performed this task hundreds of times in the past and should be able to prepare you, your bride, and the guests for all eventualities. Ask for references, and make sure to contact them! With any luck, you'll have to do an advance scouting trip of the resort in Jamaica where you're going to tie the knot. Not bad, right?

Of critical importance are passports and visas, if required, and transportation to your exotic locale. You are going to want to give your guests plenty of advance notice so that they can book flights cheaply. Furthermore, if you choose to host the wedding during the high season (typically wintertime), the rates are going to increase substantially. While you may be able to afford a high season wedding in the Caribbean, are there any potential guests of yours who could not afford to come?

A WORD ABOUT SMALL WEDDINGS

Nearly every couple, in the heat of wedding planning, wants to abandon it all and host a simple affair—the small wedding. It's a great idea that works well in theory. You invite forty to seventy-five people, book a local restaurant, have personalized wedding favors ("What are those!?"), and make the wedding an intimate affair for close family and friends. Unfortunately, it's very difficult to pull off, not because organizing this kind of wedding is problematic, but because it's virtually impossible to trim a lifetime worth of guests to forty to seventy-five people. Think of all of your friends from the various stages of your life. Think of all of your family. Multiply the number by 2.5. (Two because of you and your fiancée, and .5 because half of these guests are going to have a significant other.) You're at seventy-five already, at least. And what of relatives who have large families with many children? You get the point. By all means, try for a small wedding, but plan on something larger.

INTERFAITH CEREMONIES

Outdoors? Indoors? In Aruba? A bigger question for modern couples is what to do when two people of different religious affiliations are getting married. Have a discussion early on in wedding planning. Accommodating religion in your life is something entirely different from accommodating religion in your wedding. That's because religion is highly personal, whereas a wedding ceremony is highly public, most of the time. One important point is to avoid assuming that your fiancée knows what you (or your family) is expecting, or vice versa. It is not uncommon for people who haven't even been inside a house of worship in years to insist on getting married in one. If you're a mixed-faith couple and you both want a religious wedding, you may have to get creative within the bounds of your religion. It gets particularly tricky when trying to find a friendly religious official to officiate the ceremony. Some religions forbid mixed-faith weddings; others have no issues with it, but may have restrictions on what rituals will be permitted in the ceremony. What does virtually every religion have in common? Most will not allow photographs to be taken during the wedding ceremony.

Ordering Up a Combo

Having a "combo" ceremony means having one religion lead your wedding ceremony but having an officiant of the other religion then bless the union. This is best if, as a couple, you don't mind one religion leading the proceeding, but would like the presence of a religious leader from the "other" religion. There are many ways to try to accommodate more than one religion in your ceremony, and there are many interfaith versions of traditionally religious rituals. For example, the Jewish *Ketubah*, a contract that bride and groom usually sign in a religious ceremony, can be found in a nondenomi-national or interdenominational form.

Losing Faith?

If your wedding ceremony plans are leaving you feeling a bit dazed, you may want to scrap them alto-gether and select to have the wedding in a secular venue. Even though you may want a priest or rabbi to bless the wedding, you may not feel the need to have the ceremony in a house of worship. This might be something that her family will be far more comfort-able with if they practice a different religion.

Furthermore, you can have a spiritual but non-specific ceremony. If you avoid tension-building situations and theological language, you might be able to focus better on the importance of the cer-emony, which is the union of two people in love (followed by a *wicked* party).

YOUR WEDDING BUDGET

Setting your wedding budget brings out the inner financial planner and accountant in both you and your fiancée. You'll be unpleasantly surprised to know that the average American wedding is creep-ing upwards of $25,000 on average. How much your wedding will cost is directly contingent on how much your income allows you to spend and whether you're receiving cash from family. If you want to host a $5,000 wedding, you're going to host a small wedding for fifty to seventy-five guests. Squeeze in 100 guests, and all of the sudden it's less lavish. At a minimum, you'll spend about $3,000 on a wedding, but that will be a small, barebones, local wedding. It can be done on such a budget by cutting costs, particularly in the exceedingly expensive wedding reception. However, even a wedding held in your backyard will cost you a fair amount of money if you need to hire catering staff.

Who Pays Nowadays?

Gone are the days when your father-in-law would underwrite the costs of the entire wedding or even the wedding reception. It's the twenty-first century, and now the groom's family is pitching in. Furthermore, today more brides and grooms are paying for the wedding themselves, with limited financial contribution from the parents. If your parents are helping with the wedding costs, the power of the purse strings may entail a venue and menu veto, as well as a say in the music and even power to invite guests whom neither you nor your bride have ever met.

Traditional Cost Breakdown

Based on tradition that began in Moses' time (or something akin to that), here is a list of who covers what:

Your Glorious Fiancée and Her Family

- The engagement party
- The groom's ring
- Wedding gown and accessories
- Gifts for the bridal party
- Gift for the groom
- Invitation, wedding announcements, ceremony, reception programs, and thank-you cards
- Ceremony site rental
- Decorations for the ceremony site
- Wedding entertainment
- Bridal wedding-day gown
- Ceremony fees
- The photographer
- Reception costs including music, food, drink, and decorations
- All flowers, except for flowers worn by the groom, fathers, grandfathers, and male attendants

You and Your Family

- Cost of the honeymoon
- Marriage license
- Rehearsal dinner
- Officiant's fees
- Your attire
- Gift for the bride
- Gifts for the male attendants
- Wedding transportation expenses on the day of the wedding

- Boutonnieres for the male attendants, including both fathers and grandfathers
- Bride's engagement and wedding rings

What about Income Disparities?

Your parents might be living the American dream. They have 2.5 children and a nice house in the suburbs, and are a couple of years away from retirement. They have given their children every opportunity, and the children have succeeded. Because of their efforts, you and your wife make more money than your parents do. Who pays for the wedding?

If You Make More Than Your Parents

Frankly, you should offer to cover the costs. In addition to ensuring the wedding you want, this approach is realistic. Why make your parents (or your in-laws) take a second mortgage on the house or dip into savings when you and your bride would only have to tighten your belts a bit? If you have the funds ready to pay and the parents do not, we suggest that you should offer to pay.

If One Set of Parents Is Wealthier Than the Other

In another alternative, your fiancée's parents want to contribute or pay outright, but your parents make substantially more money. We believe there is nothing wrong with the groom's parents saying that "tradition is ridiculous." It doesn't matter that in other circumstances they'd be happy to let the bride's parents fork over the cash—scrapping tradition in favor of expediency is the right choice.

If Your Parents Have Similar Levels of Income

If both sets of parents have similar levels of income, it's a lot easier for the groom and bride to convince each other's parents to assist with costs. If the bride and groom prepare a proper budget, it becomes much easier to manage expectations and to assign payment responsibilities and timing of payments. In sum, communication and tact are key. We believe that the modern bride and groom should be prepared to pay a portion of the costs.

PREMARITAL COUNSELING

"Counseling? Already?" you may ask. In fact, it's not a bad idea to seek premarital counseling, and doing so is not defeatism or a sign of marital weakness that needs to be "fixed" before the Wedding March is pumped over the church organs. Premarital counseling is a chance for the bride and groom to meet with a professional therapist, lay out any issues on the proverbial "couch," and dig into the actual and potential issues that every relationship faces. If you've read the first chapter of this book and considered the Ten Tough Questions that pose potential problems for newlyweds, you've already digested the idea that a marriage is something quite apart from a wedding. (And after you get married, you'll understand why people say that a marriage is hard work.)

Indeed, you may have discovered that you can't reserve a church or synagogue for your wedding ceremony without first taking a marriage preparation class. The benefit of a preparation course or any other form of premarital counseling is the potential to reduce the risk of divorce, lead to a significantly happier marriage, and help reduce the stress of merging two families together. You'll be surprised at what issues surface now. Marriage preparation will teach you and your fiancée how to deal with these issues so that they don't become toxic to your relationship.

PRENUPTIAL AGREEMENTS

Nothing can kill romance faster than those two words: "prenuptial agreement." The "prenup" is a contract between two people that outlines how assets will be distributed in the event of divorce or death. Prenups have been around for thousands of years among royalty in Europe and Asia, who needed to protect their family's wealth and namesake.

Only 5 percent of couples getting married for the first time and 20 percent of couples preparing for their second marriage will enter into prenuptial agreements. It is only a useful tool when one party to the marriage has substantially more assets than the other, or together the couple brings into the marriage substantial assets that are likely to grow.

Of course, it is hard (and off-putting) to think about divorce in the midst of making a lifelong commitment, and it probably seems defeatist. However, you've heard the startling statistics regarding divorce. Furthermore, did you know that your spouse might be entitled to a significant percent of your future earnings if she supported you in some way? This may be as small as giving you money for groceries while you were starving through business school. There are mathematical formulas that divorce lawyers use to calculate the value of professional credentials in terms of the amount of money that you will make during your entire working life.

Accordingly, prenuptial agreements protect your assets, prevent controversies during a divorce, and reveal the financial condition of your future spouse. If you are in the position where you could be on the hook for spousal maintenance, it is something to consider as part of financial planning.

four

Pre-Game Prep

NOW THAT EVERYONE knows about the engagement, a date has been set, and a budget has been decided upon, it's time to celebrate! In this chapter, we discuss the engagement party (whether to have one) as well as stag and doe parties (putting the word "fun" into wedding fundraising). More importantly, we discuss how to deal with Bridezilla if she rears her fire-breathing head.

THE ENGAGEMENT PARTY

Engagements are cause for celebration, and therefore you or your fiancée may wish to throw an engagement party for yourselves. The engagement party is usually a casual, relaxed affair with your closest friends and family: jeans, instead of tuxedos, and plenty of appetizers and drinks. An engagement party is certainly not required, but it can be a lot of fun. Typically, the engagement party is held a few months after the proposal and generally no later than six months before the wedding date.

The engagement party may informally bring together two families who might not otherwise have had the opportunity to meet. Your brothers get to meet her sisters; her mom meets your father, and so on. It will make the wedding day less awkward as your brothers link arms with a bridesmaid they've actually spoken to.

TIPS FOR THE SMART GROOM

To avoid paying for extra postage, make sure that your invitations are standard letter size. To save additional money, skip the traditional self-addressed, postage-paid RSVP cards, and ask guests to RSVP via phone or e-mail. Eliminating the bulky RSVP cards and their accompanying envelopes will also reduce the weight of your invitations, which ensures that you don't pay extra postage for any extra weight.

The engagement party can also be a way to celebrate your wedding for those that aren't likely to attend the wedding, or for those to whom you might not extend a formal invitation. For example, you might have several work acquaintances with whom you might golf with from time to time but who wouldn't be on a trimmed-down guest list. Co-workers will appreciate the opportunity to celebrate your marriage in this more intimate manner. If you're not planning on inviting some or all of them to your wedding, this is your opportunity to tell them that you're hosting an engagement party as your wedding may be a "smaller event."

The engagement party can be used as a fundraiser for the bride and groom, similar to what is called a "stag and doe party." A stag and doe is typically a slightly rowdier affair than the average engagement party. An engagement party is a get-together, whereas a stag and doe party is designed primarily to assist the bride and groom pay for their wedding.

FUNDRAISING: THE STAG AND DOE PARTY

With weddings costing a fortune, it's not a bad idea for the couple to consider hosting a stag and doe party. No one will be under the impression you're hosting it only so as to have a good time. No, the stag and doe party exists to finance a portion of your wedding expenses. Some may find the concept to be a bit crass, but if done right, it's well worth it for you and great fun for a Saturday night. It does require a lot of planning (as if more planning was needed in this wedding planning process).

When it comes to a stag and doe party, the name of the game is throwing a fantastic party and (no sugar coating here) making money. There are three essential ways to accomplish this task:

- Selling tickets to the party
- Selling drinks with a slight margin for you
- Providing games to separate people from their cash

The tickets will be your primary source of income. Ten to fifteen dollars is a good range. The idea is to have as many people as possible attend. Any higher than fifteen dollars, and you are making your party more expensive than the latest blockbuster movie!

Location, Location, Location

An easy location for the party is at a bar or club. The establishment is likely to insist (for either business or licensing reasons) that you use their bartenders and allow them to sell the alcohol. If that is the case, you will have to arrange a profit-sharing deal with that fine drinking institution, and many are only too happy to comply. Ideally, you want to supply your own alcohol so that all the monetary proceeds come directly back to you. Check into what permits you may need where you live. While you should provide free food—appetizers and snacks, mostly—your guests should be expected to pay for their own drinks. Budget for approximately four drinks per guest. Be sure to stock up on beer and wine, as you'll want to be able to accommodate many tastes.

Keep 'Em Entertained

At the event, you will want to plan more ways to keep the guests entertained (with the side benefit of raising more money). Fortunately, this is an easy task. Pool tournaments, karaoke, darts, billiards tournaments, card games, mechanical bulls, and inflatable sumo wrestling suits are great ways to keep your guests happy and generate funds. Offer a fifty-fifty split on any activity—whoever wins gets half the prize money, and you get the other half.

Stag and doe parties are a great way to raise money while having a good time. It's also a great way to be inclusive, as not everyone you know can be invited to your wedding. Furthermore, your friends will want to invite their friends. The more the merrier. Enlist the help of your best man and groomsmen to make the party go off without a hitch. Of course, you'll need to have someone at the door, someone serving drinks, someone replenishing the food, and someone doing regular sweeps of the room to collect empty glasses and trash. Keep the drinks flowing, the music playing, and try to personally thank every guest for coming to ensure that spirits stay high. Execute this party well, and the whole night will be a great success. As an added bonus, the stag and doe will contribute greatly to your bride's budget for flowers.

DEALING WITH BRIDEZILLA

Imagine Godzilla devastating a skyline inhabited by innocent civilians. Now picture your fiancée leaving a trail of shredded wedding invitations, astronomical cell phone bills, and pools of tears in her wake. Combine the two, and you've got Bridezilla on your hands. Bridezilla is born, Bridezilla has risen, Bridezilla is real, and you must act to rescue her from her own devastating wrath. It doesn't have to be this way. How can this beast be stopped? How can you avoid getting trampled under her thunderous footfall? With a little finesse, you can be part of the solution.

How Do You Know When She Has . . . Mutated?

Trust us on this one . . . you'll know! Your usually composed, even-tempered partner will become suddenly obsessed with the wedding plans, seemingly focusing day and night on little else. She will, at times, become irritable, accusatory, dismissive, irrational, and demanding. It's not PMS (and in fact, never speak those three letters aloud), it's the biggest day of her life, and dammit, it's going to be flawless. As the groom, you'll need to be patient.

Emotions are in flux and stress is at an all-time high. Why? Because in addition to the rigors of work, you've just added planning the most important event of your lives. She wants perfection.

How Do You Cope?

The name of the game is prevention before implosion. Before you've reached the planning stages of your wedding, discuss with your bride-to-be about how the two of you plan to tackle the responsibility. Talk about what each of you will be responsible for, and make a pact not to let the enormity of the task ahead get the best of you.

And remember: you're not guilty . . . unless you are. It's up to you to uphold your end of the bargain, which is really all a smart groom can do. If you drop the ball, know that you will incur the wrath of Bridezilla. To avoid any unwanted surprises and resentment, write out the division of responsibilities. See Chapter 5 for our list of the groom's duties.

Maybe Money Is the Issue?

Money problems may be occupying her thoughts. She might be bent on personalized party favors from Tiffany & Co. This is a good opportunity to remind her of the mantra that this wedding is really about celebrating the two of you, and not spending an arm and leg on things that are disposable.

TIPS FOR THE SMART GROOM

When in doubt, change her screensaver to your honeymoon destination to remind her that there is light at the end of the tunnel. Buy her a travel guide to wherever it is that you are going.

"What Can I Do?"

If you hear her complain about the work involved in wedding preparations, just use these magic words to solve your dilemma: "What can I do?" Your Bridezilla will be pleased to hear it, and will either take you up on your offer or go back to her crazed planning with the knowledge that at least you care.

Eat, Drink, and Be Married

If all your verbal attempts to be there for your Bridezilla fail, take action. Suggest a weekend getaway, a day trip, or even a romantic night out to get her mind off of flower arrangements. A glass of wine does wonders after any workday.

YOUR WIFE'S NAME CHANGE

Marriage brings about changes that can be dramatic for you and your fiancée. In your case, it may be the first time in your life that you wear gold jewelry.

(Yes, we know that's a big deal.) But for your fiancée, it's a different story. If your wife changes her name to yours, she loses a piece of her past identity, and may even feel like she's lost a lot of it.

Taking Your Name

The traditional option is to adopt your surname. This will take time for her to get used to, especially if she is fond of her family name. As most men would hesitate to take on their fiancée's name, you should expect some hesitation from your fiancée. A significant logistical headache is changing her name on all existing bank and credit accounts, insurance policies, and identification. It's kind of like losing your wallet. Her name change is a tedious task for her, but services such as Miss-NowMrs.com can ease the transition by helping clients change their Social Security number, U.S. passport, address, driver's license. They can also help you obtain certified marriage certificates.

The-Hyphenated-Option-Can-Work

The hyphenated option is a possible compromise for those women who wish to state that they have joined your family (in spirit) but also still maintain their former identity. For women with established careers, this option is understandable, given their existing name recognition. Be gracious that she wants your name on anything associated with her!

No Change at All

The no-change option may disappoint you. If your fiancée has suggested that she's "just going to keep my own name," you're either up for *battle royale* or a calm discussion and compromise. You can't force your new wife to take your name, although you *can* ask. It doesn't particularly matter if you've got a simple name like Jones or a long Greek name that includes every vowel in the alphabet. After all, we know that you wouldn't change your name. Your bride-to-be will vow to spend the rest of her life with you. That should be of much greater significance.

Ever Thought of Changing Your Name?

If you've thought about being asked to change your last name to hers, you'll gain an appreciation why your fiancée's last name is important to her and why she may be reluctant to do so.

five

What Does a Groom Have to Do?

THINK BEEMERS OR stretch limos, not flowers. Planning a wedding is a large undertaking. While we recognize that the bride is going to plan out the majority of the event, there are plenty of things that you need to do to get across the finish line. Some of the planning can be delegated. For example, if you're not an aesthetically minded guy, it's okay to delegate flower selection and other decorations to your fiancée. However, you're not just along for the ride. Major decisions like the budget, size, and venue of the wedding should not be decided by just one person. You and your fiancée should sit down and talk these things through to see what you both have in mind. If you have open communication, it will save you both from unleashing Bridezilla.

A GROOM'S SPECIFIC TASKS

There are several tasks that are specific to the groom. These tasks define your contribution to the wedding and are traditionally held as crucial to fulfilling your role as a groom. You'll need to show initiative and handle your groom responsibilities respectably. Here's a quick list of responsibilities that will almost certainly fall on your shoulders:

- Learning about diamond engagement rings and buying one
- Saving for a diamond engagement ring
- Choosing your wedding party
- Selecting wedding attire for the men in the wedding party
- Arranging transportation to the ceremony for the bride, the father of the bride, the bridal party, the best man, the groomsmen, and yourself
- Arranging transportation for the entire wedding party from the ceremony to the reception (A hint: You'll be arriving separately from your wife, but leaving as a couple.)
- Arranging for accommodations for out-of-town guests
- Purchasing a gift for your bride-to-be ("What, another gift?!")
- Purchasing gifts for your groomsmen

- Obtaining a marriage license
- Planning the rehearsal dinner
- Preparing a toast for the rehearsal dinner
- Preparing a speech for the reception
- Planning the honeymoon

You should consider handling these tasks by yourself as they are fairly painless ways to arrange major parts of the wedding experience and avoid putting all the pressure on your fiancée. There's a whole host of things that you and your fiancée can do together. You should always feel free to do more—it's your wedding too, after all, and seeing how involved you are in this event is sure to make your fiancée glad she picked you. If nothing else, work with her to do the following:

- Set wedding budget and size
- Finalize a date, time, and location and book the reservations
- Select the officiant, if you are not having a religious wedding
- Book a reception site
- Settle on a wedding theme and style for your reception
- Book entertainment
- Draft a guest list (this will be time consuming)
- Select and order invitations

- Mail out invitations
- Plan the reception menu
- Hire a photographer
- Create a gift registry

If you only had one job throughout this entire process, it would be this: No matter how crazy the planning gets, never forget the mantra that this wedding is about celebrating the love between you and your fiancée. Get involved, have your say on the floral arrangements if you can bear it, and get your marriage started in the most positive light possible.

TIPS FOR THE SMART GROOM

To save on flower or decoration costs, choose ceremony and reception sites that are already ornate. A hotel ballroom and an elaborate church, for example, will not require much decorating.

WEDDING FLOWERS
ARE NOT YOUR PROBLEM

While you might be dragged along kicking and screaming by your fiancée as she shops for flowers, there's really only one flower that you need to care about: the boutonniere (pronounced: boo-tin-neer).

Many grooms and groomsmen wear boutonnieres, which is the only flower a groom needs to think about at all. Just as most brides and bridesmaids carry floral bouquets, a boutonniere is a flower that is specially made to be worn on the lapel of the groom and groomsmen, and is typically a rose in a particular color (or possibly a daisy). You might have some say in what flower will be used for the boutonniere, and you have a veto over any flower that you think will look ridiculous on your lapel.

TIPS FOR THE SMART GROOM

Traditionally, the groom pins a corsage (a bouton-niere, but for women) on his mother on the day of the wedding. It is a nice gesture and good wedding etiquette.

Boutonnieres can be a nice touch and a nod to the glorious bridesmaids as they can be matched with the bride's and bridesmaids' flowers or dresses. The bride typically arranges the purchase of boutonnieres and corsages when she arranges wedding flowers. Importantly, the boutonnieres are delivered to the groom on the morning of the wedding, so the groom is responsible for making it a smooth delivery.

If you are driving to the wedding and wearing a boutonniere, be careful with that seatbelt. They have a tendency to decapitate boutonnieres. Obviously, wear your seatbelt, but just make sure to take off the boutonniere.

Flowers. That's about all you'll need to know. Put the book down for a while, and go tell your fiancée why you love her.

THE SECOND AND THIRD WEDDING RINGS

There are three rings involved in the wedding. The first, which provides the most shine, is the engagement ring. The next two rings are the wedding rings themselves. First, the good news: They don't cost very much money. In fact, you can get two nondiamond wedding rings for you and for your bride for less than $2,000, and even that is on the expensive side. Now that you've got the diamond ring, discuss the budget you can afford with your fiancée and encourage her to choose her wedding ring. Women often want to have a platinum ring with no diamonds. For you, choose a ring that feels good on your finger and that is wide enough. You'll want to go with at least 14 karat gold or platinum so that it is strong and not prone to denting or scratching. One inexpensive alternative is tungsten, which, due to its hardness, is scratchproof and will shine forever as it did on your wedding day. Skip titanium, which has a tendency to scuff very easily. Buying the wedding rings is a great special date night opportunity for you. Plan it for about six to eight weeks before your wedding day.

MARRIAGE LICENSES MADE EASY

Marriage is inherently personal, but nonetheless the government wants to be made aware of your plans. This is easily accomplished through the marriage license, which requires you to provide a copy of your birth certificates and cash payment, and often requires you and your fiancée's presence in order to have your marriage recognized by the state. To add more mystery, if you are planning a destination wedding (be it to Aruba or Wyoming), you should check what rules and procedures are in place in order to have the government recognize your marriage. The smart groom will get the licensing details out of the way in the weeks prior to the wedding day.

On wedding day, you will receive a marriage certificate, which will be signed after the ceremony by an officiant and a witness. This certificate is important in proving to the government that you were married, and is used for travel, tax, and other legal purposes. The marriage certificate itself will be requested from time to time during your married life.

GETTING FIT FOR THE BIG DAY— AND BEYOND

The pictures taken on wedding day will be etched in digital memory. While it's natural to want to be a bit more trim and fit for your wedding day, it's probably a better idea for you to consider making a lifestyle change. If you've come out of college carrying a lot more baggage than you had going in, maybe it's time to get back into sports that don't involve beer. And in fact, you may have a willing partner in your fiancée. There's no better time to make a lifestyle change than when planning for a wedding.

Whether you or your fiancée (or both of you) are a bit out of shape, the secret is to get into shape together through some form of cardiovascular activity. Nothing motivates like a 10-kilometer running race in the spring before your summer wedding. Why not express to your fiancée a desire that "you've always had" to be healthy and physically fit?

With some subtlety and sensitivity, there is no reason that you shouldn't be able to encourage her without hurting her feelings or stressing her out. Remember, she wants even more than you do to look fabulous, so you may be surprised just how receptive she is to having you help her along the way.

The trick is to find the right tool for the job. Yoga ("What's that?!") or Pilates are great ways of reducing stress and can be done as a couple. Co-ed team sports through community leagues will also produce results, albeit slowly. Find an activity that you both enjoy, and make it a regular part of your weekly schedule. It's a very cheap date night.

Of course, if you plan to embark on any kind of fitness plan, be sure to save a tuxedo fitting until closer to the wedding day. If you get measured for a tuxedo in December, for example, and then diligently work out for the next three months, be prepared to have a different physique by March and an ill-fitting rental.

With a bit of work, and support from your bride, you can look like a fit groom on wedding day. Nothing will feel better than your old friends coming up to congratulate you on getting married to your beautiful bride, and asking, "Have you been working out?"

six

Picking Your Team: The Best Man and Groomsmen

CHOICES, CHOICES. IN this chapter, we focus on the choices that the prospective groom has to make, including choosing a best man, groomsmen, and wedding MC (Master of Ceremonies).

DEFINING THE BEST—MAN, THAT IS

When it comes to the wedding, the second most important person for the groom is the best man. (If you have to guess at who is the most important person for the groom, we've lost you already.) The best man will be taking an active role before, during, and after the wedding. Being the best man is a great honor for him, but there's a lot of responsibility resting on his shoulders.

So Who's It Gonna Be?

Take a short trip down memory lane, and it becomes obvious. It could be the younger brother you used to beat up (and, though you would never admit to it, is a much better basketball player than you). It could be your college roommate (and former wingman). It could be your best friend from high school. The choice is very personal, but probably obvious to you. You can only pick one best man. Above all, he (or, in this modern age, possibly even a *she*) has to be a very responsible guy.

RESPONSIBILITIES OF A RESPONSIBLE GUY

No matter who gets the nod, you'll want to lay out for your best man the responsibilities of the position. Your bride will appreciate you doing this, particularly if she doesn't really like your best man. (Hey, it can happen.) You'll know you've got your man if you both believe that he can accomplish the tasks described in the following sections.

Months Before the Wedding

In the months before the wedding, the best man will:

- Organize either a mild or wild bachelor party for you, and keep you out of the doghouse in doing so;
- Get fitted for a tuxedo, on time;

- Be on time for the wedding, and get you there on time too;
- Help you with your wedding duties;
- Make a wedding toast; and
- Be your confidant.

Days Before the Wedding

If he's traveling from afar, you'll be very happy to see your best man arriving in one piece at the airport. The days before the wedding are a great time to catch up with your best man. Aside from getting there on time, the best man will:

- Attend the rehearsal and rehearsal dinner;
- Help decorate the reception site with flowers, boughs, and other frilly things that the bride came up with;
- Help decorate the wedding transportation, if necessary; and
- Liaise with the wedding MC about how the reception should flow.

In Preparation for the Ceremony

When the big day comes, your best man will:

- Help you get dressed in your tuxedo and make sure you arrive at the ceremony on time (about thirty minutes before the wedding starts);
- Keep the rings until the ring exchange;

- Sign the marriage certificate and act as a legal witness to the marriage;
- Help the photographer gather and organize the guests for any group shots;
- Have umbrellas in case it rains;
- Have a plan in case the transportation does not arrive or is late; and
- Take the initiative in case things go awry.

TIPS FOR THE SMART GROOM

Let's say the best man is your best friend from college, and he brings his current girlfriend or perhaps his wife. The smart bride and groom are courteous and seat this person in a nice spot at a table and introduce her to some friends. Remember, she's not likely to know too many people at your wedding, but she's an important person to your best man.

His Duties at the Reception

Above all else, the best man, together with the wedding MC, runs the reception. Are the caterers about to serve the wrong course? Guess who jumps up to correct the error while the MC makes some jokes? Did Uncle Tom have a bit too much to drink? Guess who brings him up to his room? The best man acts to keep any unfortunate incidents out of the sight of the bride. You'll return the favor one day.

More visibly, the best man is typically called upon to make a wedding toast to the groom. Check out GroomGroove.com for videos and articles about helping the best man get off the podium alive.

Post-Reception

The best man's responsibilities don't end when you and your bride drive off into the sunset. He must do some wrapping up before he can leave too. You best man should:

- Help load and transport and secure the wedding gifts from the reception site;
- Make sure that nothing is left at the reception site;
- If needed, drive you newlyweds to the airport, home, or to your hotel;
- Return both your tuxedo and his.

In sum, the role of the best man is not ceremonial. The best man's job is to solve any problems that arise (within reason), make sure you get to the wedding site on time, and soothe any jitters you might have.

CHOOSING THE GROOMSMEN

The groomsmen are not expendable. They are the crew that takes care of you during the wedding ceremony and preceding events. They are also matched by the same number of bridesmaids.

> ### TIPS FOR THE SMART GROOM
>
> Once you're done reading this chapter, put the book down, and go send your fiancée an e-mail or text message to tell her you love her. Better yet, give her a big hug. There are big bonus points for random acts like this.

How Many Groomsmen Will You Have?

You'll need an equal number of groomsmen to match the bridesmaids. That typically means between two to three groomsmen, plus a best man. No, you can't have more or fewer groomsmen than your bride has bridesmaids.

Your Roster of Gentlemen

So who gets the nod to be your groomsmen? First, you should consider your family. A sibling might be a good choice, particularly if the role of best man went to your best friend. You should not feel pressure to include your brothers if you don't want to or if there are large age differences. (Typically, a groomsman will not be under the age of eighteen.) You may want to consider including one of your soon-to-be brothers-in-law if your fiancée has any. If there are two or more qualified brothers-in-law, then let your fiancée make the decision, or don't pick any of them at all.

TIPS FOR THE SMART GROOM

Children make for perfect ring presenters during the wedding ceremony. If you have many young relatives, ask their parents if they would be appropriate for that duty. Not only will the children love being involved, but it's fun to include children in your ceremony because you never know what will happen! Don't trust the wedding rings with the ring bearers, even though that may seem counterintuitive. The best man holds the rings.

You want groomsmen who are responsible, punctual, and affable. Your college friend would be great if only he wasn't forgetful and a tad irresponsible. You want him to collect his tuxedo on time. When you ask someone to stand up in your wedding, be sure to explain what is expected of him. You should also be sensitive to his financial situations. You need to make sure he can afford to pay for the tuxedo rental and hotel accommodations. A good groomsman will be able to:

- Attend the wedding, including travel and accommodation costs;
- Attend the rehearsal and dinner;
- Rent a tuxedo on time;
- Assist with planning and attending the bachelor party;
- Act as an usher and seat guests at the wedding;
- Stand there and not faint, dammit;
- Walk down the aisle with a bridesmaid when the ceremony is done;
- Dance with the same bridesmaid; and
- Buy you and your bride a spectacular wedding gift.

CHOOSING A MASTER OF CEREMONIES

The perfect Master of Ceremonies (MC) is an enthusiastic friend who already has a great sense of self-worth often maintained through frequent public performances. Your local politician or the life of the party would make for a fine candidate. The bride and groom usually choose an MC together, pooling their list of friends. MCs are funny, outgoing, and confident people and, believe it or not, are the face of your wedding reception. Once you have selected the MC, you and your fiancée should sit down with him or her and talk about the reception. How would you like the MC to perform this role? You don't want to choose an MC who will make your bride's big day into his or her coming out as a comic that, at best, would place fourth at the local comedy club's amateur night.

Defining the Master's Responsibilities

The Master of Ceremonies is responsible for a variety of tasks. Most importantly, the MC ensures that the reception flows smoothly with everyone entertained and fed. This is a lot of responsibility. While the MC will be expected to dabble in some good, lighthearted humor, he or she will not be expected to be a standup comic. Humorous stories about the newlyweds and jokes that have been altered to fit the occasion are always entertaining. If the MC is having difficulties coming up with something, he or she can always turn to the bride, you, friends, and family. As a precaution, the MC should plan to have twice as much material as he or she should need. If the MC does a stellar job, it will make the evening that much more fun, so you need to make sure that he or she is aware of the checklist of tasks at the ceremony:

- Ensuring that all audio equipment is set up, in advance
- Speaking with the couple ahead of time to see whom they would like in the receiving line
- Gathering the wedding party for the receiving line at the appropriate time
- Announcing the entrance of the bride and groom into the reception
- Introducing him or herself as the MC
- Welcoming the guests to the wedding
- Introducing everyone in the wedding party as well as the parents of the newlyweds
- Introducing the person who will say grace, if applicable
- Announcing the serving of the first course (and knowing exactly what courses will be served and when)
- Knowing when the speeches and toasts will be presented, and that the father of bride usually presents the first toast
- Reading any messages received from guests
- Proposing a toast to the people who couldn't attend the wedding
- Announcing the official departure of the couple as "husband and wife"

Keep in mind that these are general guidelines for the MC—yours can do as much or as little as you and your bride like! Make sure everyone is aware of the responsibilities that you assign to the MC. Be flexible with your MC and always make sure you and your fiancée are aware of your MC's plans. He or she will likely have an idea about how the reception should flow, so you will definitely want to meet with the MC several times before wedding day. And of course, have the MC refer to Groom-Groove.com where there are more details of how to get the job done with class and humor.

seven

Wedding Wheels, Hired Paparazzi, and Cool Tunes

ASIDE FROM CHOOSING your best man and groomsmen, believe it or not, your vote counts (on select items) when it comes to weddings. In this chapter, we'll cover wedding wheels, photographers, DJs, and the all-important but often overlooked gift registry (free stuff!).

WEDDING WHEELS

The smart groom will take charge of how you and your glorious bride will roll on wedding day. Whether it's a horse-drawn carriage, stretch limousine, or your own nicely decorated 1998 Ford Taurus, you can be in command of this decision if you volunteer for this duty. While you may never have considered that you'll need a way to roll on wedding day, wedding transportation is a big logistical piece of wedding planning. Why? At the very least, you'll need to organize special transportation to get the bride to the wedding ceremony, and to get the wedding party from the ceremony to a photo shoot and/or the reception.

There are four price-influencing factors:

1. Number of passengers,
2. Length of rental,
3. Parking,
4. What you're rolling in.

Who Gets Shuttled Around?

Traditionally, the bride and groom and the wedding party have their transportation provided for them. This is so that the wedding party can stick together for photos after the reception. Accordingly, if you've got a wedding party that includes eight people, you're going to need something that will move these folks. (It's not just because they're cool that people rent limos for wedding day . . . .) You do not have any obligation to provide transportation to any other guests. An honorable mention goes to providing special treatment for parents and grandparents. It can be a nice touch if you can afford it.

It's All about Timing

As a first order of business, you'll need transportation to drive the bride to the ceremony. Following the ceremony, the transportation will drive the wedding party to the photo site, and eventually, to the reception. In between the bride's arrival and the arrival at the reception, there's a lot of waiting time. This can be quite expensive, but unavoidable. Most wedding transportation providers have a four-hour minimum rental, and you're going to need four hours anyway.

Mode of Transportation

The mode of transportation reflects your wedding theme and even your personal style. There are plenty of options to consider.

Classic White Stretch Limousine

The white limo is a wedding icon. Typically a Cadillac or Lincoln Town Car converted into a stretch, the white limo is also an icon for high school prom. Nevertheless, there is no single better way to keep the wedding party together than a white limo seating six to eight passengers.

Horse-Drawn Carriage

This is every girl's dream, but slightly smelly and impractical unless you live near New York's Central Park or have access to horses with frilly carriages. That said, it's still worth considering if it'll make your bride happy.

Vintage or Antique Cars

Think Pontiac Bonnevilles, Rolls-Royce Silver Clouds, or Ford Model Ts. Very cool rides, but a hard score. Your local wedding transportation company may offer a very small selection of vintage cars for you. Unfortunately, this will require some work, as you'll have to call around. Classic cars are not as abundant as white stretch Lincoln Town Cars. And while the local antique car club seems like a great option, most antique cars have insurance policies that prevent them from being rented out for commercial purposes. Give it a try, however, because a vintage or antique car makes for a great wedding day ride.

Sports Cars

Unless you already own a Beemer and get it serviced regularly at your local dealership, it's going to be very hard to secure two or more exotic or sports cars for wedding day. You're likely going to have to start with your local wedding transportation company, though most of the time these companies won't have much in terms of selection, nor will they likely have two or three matching cars. Consider yourself lucky if it works out that way for you. Alternatively, you can go right to your local dealer. However, dealers generally won't rent these out (or allow for "extended test drives").

Stretch SUVs

The guys at GroomGroove.com think that guys who rent stretch SUVs are trying to prove something. Save these for the bachelor party (or not at all, as they're rotten for the environment). One thing the smart groom wants to avoid is a really big SUV overshadowing his glorious bride. Because if you rent a stretch SUV, that's all the guests are going to gab about.

A Double-Decker Bus or a Trolley

These make for a great way to transport the wedding guests from the ceremony to the reception. If the wedding is about your guests, and not just you, this makes for the coolest wedding transportation of all. Check with your local tour operator.

Your Own Car

There's no shame in driving a getaway car after that happens to double as the car you use to get to work. That said, if you're going to rely on your own wheels, make sure to get the interior really clean (as your bride's dress won't take well to stains from last week's Big Mac and Fries). Furthermore, buy a special pen that writes on windows at your local art supply or hobby store, and write "Just Married" or whatever you want on your wheels. Properly decorated (by your best man or otherwise), you can turn your rust bucket into a nice and cost-effective ride for wedding day.

If you're not using your own vehicle, remember to book your transportation at least four months in advance. Stipulate the make and color of your vehicles in the contract. Ask about the company's insurance policy and whether it is licensed in your state or province. Get the best price by calling around, but avoid haggling too much on price or you'll end up saving $100 but getting an early 90s, rusty, white limo. As an extra precaution, have your best man call the car company the day before the wedding to confirm these details. At that point, all you have to do is enjoy the ride.

YOUR HIRED PAPARAZZI

When you're reminiscing about your wedding, you're likely only to have faint memories of making your vows, with slightly more memories of the honeymoon. Wedding photos are really the only artifacts you'll have. That means you should take charge, pick a quality photographer, and meet with him or her to discuss key photos in advance.

TIPS FOR THE SMART GROOM

If you are hosting a reception, you should consider booking everything with a hotel or a restaurant. Many hotels and high-end restaurants offer all-inclusive wedding packages that include tables, cutlery, room setup fees, meals, and servers. Best of all, a hotel or high-end restaurant can provide a reception that is both easy and affordable to organize. Rather than searching and paying for individual vendors (such as caterers and servers), the hotel takes care of it all for you. An added bonus is that you will only have one bill to pay and be able to budget all of the costs in advance.

Uncle Tom, Amateur Photographer

Don't hire a family member to take your wedding pictures; hire a professional. Just as you wouldn't hire an amateur plumber or doctor, don't hire an amateur photographer, or you'll end up with amateur photographs. Memories fade, but photos with bad lighting, chopped off heads, and other signs of poor photography last forever.

Shop Around

Shop around to ensure that you get the photos that you want and to avoid overpaying for a mediocre photographer. Shopping around should be done well in advance of wedding season, as photographers (along with venues) are the first to be booked. If you're looking for a photographer at an April wedding fair, it's probably a bit late for wedding season that year.

A Picture Is Worth a Thousand . . . Dollars?

Try to get price estimates from at least three professional photographers before making financial arrangements. Review your candidates' portfolios and ask for a reference. Walk away from a photographer who hesitates or refuses to provide a contact. Be sure to contact the references, and ask,

- Was the photographer easy to work with?
- Was the couple pleased with the final pictures?
- Were there any hidden costs?
- Would they hire the photographer again?

Get What You Want

Be specific with your photographer. The more specific you are with your expectations, the more accurate an estimate the photographer can give you. Furthermore, getting an estimate helps to prevent your photographer from charging extra for unwanted shots. You could, however, save money by hiring a professional photographer for the formal photo session but enlisting a friend or two to take candid shots at the reception, or even by putting disposable cameras on every table at the reception for guests to use.

TIPS FOR THE SMART GROOM

Wedding insurance, like car insurance, covers certain defined events. In the case of wedding insurance, this can include unfortunate events related to your wedding, ranging from the mundane (bad weather) to the very crappy (your photographer goes out of business). Some providers of this insurance also provide liability insurance to cover events such as when Litigation Larry slips on spilled champagne on the dance floor, breaks his back, and comes after you. The cost involved in taking out a policy differs, but we've found policies for less than $200. Check out *www.wedsafe.com* for more information.

Your photographer should provide you with a model contract for wedding photographs. Read it carefully, and make sure to add in the things that you want to have covered. If your photographer doesn't offer a written contract, you should insist on it, or write your own online. Conducting your business by e-mail can be evidence of your contractual obligations. Your contract should cover terms including:

- Price terms;
- Key information (such as where the photographer needs to show up, and when);
- Key contact information (such as cell phone numbers);
- Information on negatives (whether the price includes the negatives, or a DVD or CD of the photos);
- Use of your photos in promotional materials;
- Photos you absolutely must have; and
- Cancellation and no-show policies.

That being said, the idea is not to build a legal case for suing your wedding photographer (as a lawsuit is not going to cure your wife's anger at mediocre wedding photographs). Plan as much as you can for contingencies, and make clear what you want, when you want it, and where. That's being a smart groom. You and your bride will feel much more comfortable knowing that even if it pours you'll still have digital or print memories of your wedding day.

Flashing Lights on the Big Day

On the day of the ceremony, the photographer will be present before, during, and after the wedding ceremony, and possibly at the reception. On wedding day, you or your bride may want to have your wedding photographer take pictures of her as she gets ready for the ceremony. You may want the photos taken to be informal and not posed so as to capture the event and tell a story. Grooms should check in advance with the priest, rabbi, or officiant performing the ceremony as to whether photos can be taken during the wedding, and this information should be passed on to your photographer. More often than not, photographs are not permitted during the ceremony itself.

After the ceremony, your guests will make their way to the reception. It is usually during this time that staged photos take place at some predetermined location. If transportation is required, the smart groom will have covered this long ago. (It's unlikely that the bride in her wedding dress—or her grandmother—will want to hike six blocks.) If at all possible, try to have wedding photographs taken near the ceremony location or the reception itself.

CHOOSING RECEPTION MUSIC

Music sets the tone of your wedding reception. The success of the reception relies heavily on the music that you and your bride choose. Finding the right music can be a challenge. This is one of those tasks to tackle with your bride, especially if your idea of classical is classic rock and hers is Beethoven.

Consider the kind of music you enjoy as a couple. The genre of music should say something about you and your future wife. Don't try to satisfy everyone with Top 40 tunes, or you'll be left with a forgettable evening.

Band? DJ? String Quartet?

The reception venue can often recommend a band that has rocked the room at a previous event. A band that has worked the location before knows the dynamics of the venue, which saves a lot of hassle.

If you are hiring a DJ or musical group you haven't actually seen perform live, get a demo (video, preferably), and try to get referrals from a friend, family member, or other trusted source. Make sure the band can cater to your musical tastes. Pin down the band when it comes down to availability and reliability. Musicians can be elusive, and good bands are in demand, so book well in advance. Be warned that there are some terrible wedding singers out there ready to bring your reception down. Don't hire a family member's band unless it has a decent reputation.

Consider a string quartet or harpist for a luncheon or afternoon reception. No one will be dancing, but this will provide easy ambiance. The stringed orchestra also tends to be relatively inexpensive, which is just an added bonus.

You might want to consider the advantages of DJs, who can be more affordable than a live band, and there's no limit to the variety of music they can play. You can make list of songs that you and your fiancée would like to hear. Many DJs are moving toward laptops, making their setup time hyperquick and the amount of space needed, minimal.

"No Marilyn Manson, Please"— Make Your Expectations Clear

Whether it's a DJ or a live band, you want to remember to cover your ass. Once you've found the perfect music maker(s), get his or her signature on a contract. Usually, a band will have some sort of written contract or work order, and if they don't, you should insist on it. The contract should cover:

- Costs of performance: flat fee or hourly rate;
- Length of performance (make sure the contract with the musicians is long enough to avoid overtime. Just like your job, overtime adds up remarkably quickly);
- Cancellation policies;
- Your obligations; and
- Requirements needed at the venue.

Many factors dictate wedding music costs. For a quality band in a major city, expect to pay up to $1,000 per musician. This, of course, depends on the time of day of the performance (Can they book another performance after your reception?), how long the band or DJ is expected to play for you, and any travel costs involved or equipment rentals required. As you've read before, cutting corners generally cuts quality. The difference between incompetence and a great band may be a few hundred dollars, so start saving!

WHAT IS THE GIFT REGISTRY? SHOULD YOU CARE?

Aside from establishing your marriage and your happily-ever-after, the wedding also serves to help you acquire dishes, silverware, small appliances, and other home furnishings for free. It's a great deal. Many modern nuptials have become opportunities for indulgent materialism, and yours will not likely be different.

Large stores, from K-Mart, Wal-Mart, and Target to Williams-Sonoma and Tiffany (and everything in between), offer programs where you can preselect the items you wish to receive as gifts from your guests. This makes gift giving and getting very easy.

Armed with a scanner gun, you and your bride will spend a Sunday afternoon away from football (!), hunting through one of these stores for dishes, laundry baskets, and other "stuff." ("Do we need an espresso machine?")

You'll add items to your list, and your great-aunt in Nebraska can put away her knitting, go online, and buy gifts for you from the registry with a few clicks. It's too easy. Think of the gift registry as one big wish list, from expensive knives to towels to crock pots to sheets—which, though far from exciting, are certainly necessary. Try to select a mix of relatively inexpensive items and more expensive items so as to give your guests an opportunity to purchase off your registry without feeling like they've been had. After you and your wife return from your honeymoon, you can schedule a delivery of this treasure trove of high thread count sheets and Henckels knives.

eight

Looking Smart on Wedding Day

WHAT, EXACTLY, *IS* a cummerbund and why do people pronounce it "cumberbund"? We actually don't know why people pronounce it that way, but we *do* know that cummerbunds are almost extinct, dying out in favor of vests. Not that you care. In any event, here's a short rundown of wedding attire, including tuxedos, suits, and even beach wedding attire for the luckiest groom of them all!

WHAT YOU SHOULD WEAR

While you may be just a prop compared to your glorious bride, you (and your best man and the groomsmen) still have to dress the part. It's not easy for us guys to navigate cummerbunds, bow-ties, ascots, morning coats, and all the other foreign words associated with wedding attire for men. So let's get into it.

Match the Attire to the Affair

Unless you're lucky enough to be having a beach wedding, you'll want to dress up in some sort of formal wear for your wedding. There are several options, however, and it's not necessary that you actually wear a tuxedo. Buying a nice suit for your wedding can be a great idea, particularly if you actually need a new suit for work. Buy a suit for wedding day, and you'll have a suit to wear year round.

TIPS FOR THE SMART GROOM

One thing to consider is whether your grooms-men will wear suits that are similar to yours or exact replicas. Wearing matching suits helps with the wedding photos and purchasing coordination, but keep in mind that you're asking your grooms-men to buy the same suit, at the same price point, which they may not appreciate.

Suits can be matched easily with bridesmaids' dresses. For example, if the bridesmaids are wearing bottle green dresses, the groom and grooms-men can have bottle green matching ties and silk handkerchiefs. Your lovely fiancée will worry about that. Dark grey, navy blue, or black are all fine choices for suit colors, or, for a summer wedding, beige or linen would be ideal.

THE TRIED-AND-TRUE TUXEDO

Once you waltz into a tuxedo rental shop, you'll be amazed at the selection of rentals at your disposal. White tie or black tie; peak, notch, or shawl lapel ("Huh?"); silver ties, cummerbunds, or vests; different brands—the choices are endless. Resist the temptation to open the catalogue and pick the first thing you see.

The tuxedo jacket is the essential piece of the formal wear ensemble. Like suit jackets, these come in all sorts of styles. A typical tux jacket will be single breasted and button in the middle (as opposed to double-breasted, which wraps across your waist). There is really no difference between a tuxedo jacket and a suit jacket, with the exception of the face of the lapel, which is typically made of satin and gives it a distinct sheen. All of the regular sizes you're used to are available.

There are three styles of lapel: peak, notch, and shawl lapel. The peak lapel is the most common lapel style. It forms a V. A notch lapel is just as the name suggests—a notch is "cut out" of the lapel. The shawl lapel is a rounded, smooth lapel running from the collar down the front of the lapel. Frankly, you won't need to worry about lapel styles. (Your wedding isn't going to go down in flames because you picked a notch versus peak lapel.)

Morning Coats—and When to Wear Them

For a wedding that takes place prior to six in the evening, the proper dress for the groom is a morning coat and gray slacks (if you want to follow tradition). A morning coat is typically a full-length, single-breasted coat, distinguished by the front (which is cut back and away) and the gray striped pants that go along with it. A morning coat has a single button that buttons in the mid-waist. The morning coat is only worn with suspenders. (No cummerbund is required, thanks.) A waistcoat is worn underneath the jacket.

Top Hats

Please don't. And no canes either. That's just our opinion.

TIPS FOR THE SMART GROOM

We believe that morning coats look best on grooms and groomsmen who are taller than average, or at least not too short. The effect of the long, cut-away tail tends to make shorter grooms and groomsmen look a bit clownish, particularly if the tail of the jacket appears to be only a few inches off the ground.

Tuxedo Pants

Tuxedo pants have no cuffs. For decoration, they have a sheen satin or silk strip running on the outside of the leg—generally the same material as the front collar of the tuxedo jacket. Rental pants will have a tightening mechanism so that they can be adjusted for fit. In a custom tuxedo, the pants are held in place with suspenders and can be adjusted by a tailor.

Tuxedo Ties

The classic tuxedo is worn with a bowtie. A black bowtie, to be precise. Chances are, you have no idea how to tie a bowtie, and that's perfectly normal—it's not the kind of thing our fathers taught us. With a tuxedo rental, your package will come with a choice of ties, and most of them are pre-tied. In fact, they're not just pre-tied, they're *permanently* tied and sown to create a perfect knot. Avoid showing the elastic clip.

An alternative to the bowtie is the long tie. It is generally no different from a regular necktie, except that it will be fashioned from satin rather than from a silk weave. Long ties also come in pre-fabricated form, and the color could be dictated by your fiancée based on what her bridesmaids will be wearing. If they're wearing silver dresses, she may want you and your groomsmen to wear matching silver ties. A final alternative to the bowtie and long tie are ascots. An ascot looks slightly more formal than a bowtie or long tie. An ascot tie is a very wide tie, typically worn with a wingtip shirt collar. You'll know it when you see it.

Cufflinks and Shirt Studs

If you rent your tuxedo, a set of gold and black cufflinks and plastic shirt studs will be part of the package, and yours to lose. No need to do anything fancy, but if you want to be a bit more creative than your local tuxedo rental shop, consider going the personalized route.

You should consider purchasing high quality cufflinks as a gift for your groomsmen and best man. Instead of having the guys' nicknames or initials engraved (although that is an option), buy some Harley-Davidson cufflinks for the Harley-minded groomsman or computer chip cufflinks for the techie. Present these as a gift to the groomsmen at the rehearsal dinner.

Cummerbunds or Vests (but Not Both!)

When you open your rental tuxedo package, you're likely to discover a piece of fabric that vaguely resembles . . . a G-string for a larger woman. That's the cummerbund. It is elastic, has pleats, and looks frilly. If you're going to wear a cummerbund, remember that the pleats should open upward. (Traditionally, this was so that the pleats could hold theater tickets or catch crumbs that fell off your dinner table. Of course, it's not likely you'll open the pleats of the cummerbund after a night of partying and exclaim: "Ha! Who knew—bread crumbs!") Cummerbunds are decoration. They're not totally useless, however; if you or your best man or groomsmen are on the short side, the cummerbund may be a better option than a morning coat or a vest, as it has the effect of making you look taller.

TIPS FOR THE SMART GROOM

Never button all the buttons on your vest. As a rule, button one less than you have, and always leave the bottom button open. That goes for the tuxedo jacket as well.

In terms of a vest, you should choose between a full back (the vest covers your back) or an open back (which is flimsier though less expensive) with straps behind your neck and across your lower back.

Tuxedo Shirt

The tuxedo shirt is a critical piece of the tuxedo, as it is the one piece of the ensemble that's supposed to be comfortable (and worn closest to your skin). If you're renting a tuxedo, you're likely to receive a slightly cheap, probably starched stiff, poly-cotton blend that someone else may have worn. If you skip the cummerbund and go with a vest, you may be able to get away with not having an actual tuxedo shirt underneath as the vest and the tie will conceal most of the shirt and not reveal the shirt studs. In fact, you may be better off using one of your good white dress shirts (provided you have one that's high quality, with removable collar stays) rather than the shirt that comes with your rental. The key will be the collar stays. If you're going with a bowtie, you'll need a shirt with wingtips.

Now for the Shoes

As part of the tuxedo package, you're likely to be faced with the option of renting black, ultra-shiny, tuxedo shoes that are made of plastic and rubber. They aren't very comfortable—and by the end of the wedding day your bride isn't going to be the only one complaining of sore feet. (Buy some insoles, and you'll thank us!) Believe it or not, people notice the guys' shoes at a wedding, particularly if they aren't shiny or if everyone is wearing black patent leather shoes except one groomsman who accidentally forgot to pack them. If shoes are part of the tuxedo package, it may be easiest to use them.

But if you'd like something a bit more comfortable, use your best pair of laceup black oxford dress shoes that are well worn in. So long as they are polished to a mirror-like shine by your local shoeshine shop, they could act as a stand in. (Loafers are not allowed.)

THE GROOMSMEN'S GARB

Getting your groomsmen suited up for the wedding is a vastly more important task than figuring out the differences between a long tie, bowtie, or ascot. Why? The groom deals with the groomsman who's habitually late for events, forgetful, and likely to forget to bring his rented bowtie. Sound familiar? Getting the groomsmen fitted for formal wear is akin to herding cattle. If all of the groomsmen live in the same city where the wedding takes place, it should be fairly simple. Schedule a fitting with the groomsmen for a rainy weekend afternoon.

However, if the groomsmen are spread all over the country, your best bet is to find a national tuxedo rental chain that has an outlet in each person's hometown. A chain will be well equipped to take measurements for the exact style of tuxedo you want. The groom should ask his tuxedo rental outlet if there are deals for getting four or more tuxedos. Invariably, the store will have package deals, and frequently, the groom will get his rental for "free!" National chains often have the best deals. The average cost for a tuxedo rental for a wedding will be around $125, which includes all of the accessories the groom could possibly want. National chains may offer better discounts.

Be Prepared, Well in Advance

A few months before the wedding, you should get the essential measurements of the groomsmen, or have them get measured in person. This will invariably include neck size, shirt and pant length, and waist size. Most guys know their particular size, but it helps to be properly measured. Once the measurements are in, the smart groom only has to ensure that the tuxedos show at the rental shop a couple of days before the wedding.

nine

The Honeymoon: Your Post-Wedding Getaway

THE GOOD NEWS for you is that despite a mountain of wedding stress (for your bride of course), the names of your bride's uncles you can't quite remember, and the wedding toast you're going to make, there is light at the end of the tunnel—in the form of a memorable honeymoon. This chapter will help you prepare for the celebration of your promotion to husband. Welcome to married life! By the time you're on your honeymoon everything will be settled: You'll be newly married, the wedding will have ended, and the guests will have gone home. Life doesn't get any sweeter . . .

YOUR GREAT ESCAPE

It's a continuing tradition for the groom to plan the honeymoon. And let's be honest, who doesn't like planning a vacation? As the groom, you'll get to flex your logistical muscle so that your glorious bride can relax and contemplate clouds in the sky without ever having had to think about connecting flights and baggage allowances. You don't want anything to impede this quality time alone; honeymoons are about seclusion, sexual intimacy, romance, and a celebration of your interdependence. The best part of honeymooning is that you get to take credit for one of the most romantic parts of your relationship's story up until this point. If you can do a good job organizing the honeymoon, then you'll have some promising credibility when it comes to married life or a career as a travel agent.

HONEYMOON STYLES

Popular honeymoon styles can be categorized as follows:

- Rest and relaxation
- Cultural exploration
- Adventure honeymoons

Of course, no honeymoon fits perfectly into these boxes. For some couples, an ideal honeymoon means a tan-fest in the tropics. For others, it means watching the sunset over the Grand Canyon. And for others still, it means exploring culinary delight in a Tuscan village. In fact, you may never have considered anything *but* a beach vacation. If there's one time to do something out of the ordinary, it's your honeymoon. The world is your oyster.

TIPS FOR THE SMART GROOM

There are plenty of great spots to visit for a honeymoon that won't make your credit card squeal. For example, consider Niagara Falls, Ontario (complete with nearby wine region); Acapulco, Mexico (fun in the sun at an all-inclusive resort); a road trip (think Route 66 with an RV); Puerto Rico (less expensive than other Caribbean locales); or Yellowstone (for adventurous types).

Nontraditional Trips

More and more couples are skipping the traditional honeymoon getaways and opting for something a little more daring. We're not talking about climbing Mount Everest or heli-skiing here. You don't need to be an extreme outdoorsman to have a honeymoon that your friends will be talking about for years to come. Your adventure could be soaking up the sun on an island off the beaten path from the typical tourist destinations. Or it could be a stay at a resort that's anything but ordinary. Scubadiving on the coast of Belize? Relaxing at an ice hotel in northern Sweden? Staying right on the slopes at Whistler, Canada? These are just some ideas to mull over. Ideally, you'll find a spot that can combine adventure and relaxation. When it comes to something off the beaten path, in addition to the above-mentioned ideas the guys at GroomGroove. com suggest the following getaways.

Jamaica

It has the beach, fabulous and distinct cuisine (the home of jerk chicken), and the best coffee in the world—Blue Mountain Coffee. Many resorts will cater to destination weddings if you're not into adventure. Certain parts of Jamaica are not for the faint of heart, and accordingly, planning is required. In fact, make an advance trip when the weather is cold.

Bali

It's far away, less commercialized than similar locales, and has plenty of activities to partake in, from rafting to surfing to cultural exploration. It's paradise.

Hawaii

While Hawaii is a major honeymoon destination, skip Oahu in favor of Kau'ai, Maui, or the Big Island. Hawaii offers both modern conveniences and the possibility for seclusion and adventure as well. Learn about what each island offers. Is it possible that Hawaii was designed by God for adventurous honeymooners?

Canadian Rockies

Rockier and more remote than their U.S. brethren, the Canadian Rockies offer all the outdoor adventure you could want, and in some places—like Jasper, Alberta—without all the tourists.

Some More Ideas: A Wino's Honeymoon
San Francisco, Napa, and Sonoma
Near San Francisco, the twin valleys of Napa and Sonoma offer the very best in American cuisine, sun, scenery, culture, and of course wine. It's close enough to San Francisco to spend a week-long honeymoon in the area and not get bored.

New Zealand
A sauvignon blanc honeymoon, and bungee jumping if you're brave! New Zealand is mellow, compact, and not an overwhelming place to honeymoon. It's just the place to go to explore fine sauvignon blanc and mix it with great adventure. (The Kiwis invented bungee jumping.)

Mendoza, Argentina
For an off-the-beaten-track honeymoon with plenty of great wine, fly to Buenos Aires (and spend some

time there) and then jet over to Mendoza, *el capital* of Argentina's wine region. Argentina produces fine cabernet sauvignon and is a very affordable place to honeymoon.

COUNTDOWN TO THE HONEYMOON

You should start planning well in advance to ensure that your honeymoon delivers the reward you lovebirds deserve. You might not be able to control the weather, airlines, or accommodations, but you should take control of what is within your grasp. So what can you plan for?

TIPS FOR THE SMART GROOM

If you want to be really romantic, keep the honeymoon destination a secret from your bride until just before the honeymoon. Tell your fiancée the kind of destination on offer (beach, adventure, cultural) so that she knows what to pack. Drop hints in the months before the wedding, but keep your lips sealed. On wedding day, you'll have an extra special surprise: "We're going to Buffalo!"

When Does the Planning Start?— Agree on the Playground

Assuming you're already engaged, the right time to start on your honeymoon plans is starting six months before you actually utter your vows. If you want, consult your fiancée and try to come up with a short list of possible honeymoon destinations. You might have different ideas about what makes the perfect vacation getaway. The world's a big place, and if you do a little research, you're bound to find a destination that is satisfactory for both of you. Write a short list of possible vacation spots with advantages and disadvantages. Make sure you consider the time of year that you go on your honeymoon. Your job situation will affect the timing of your wedding and your honeymoon. The summer is better for most employees, hence the wedding season runs roughly from May to October. However, if it's sweltering in Boston, the heat is probably *melting* everything in the Caribbean. Some couples plan a summer wedding but hold off on their honeymoon until the frigid winter air descends upon them. It's your call. Furthermore, pay attention to hurricane season if you're planning a Caribbean getaway. Hurricane season extends from early June until November. Even if there's no hurricane on the horizon, you may be stuck with rainy weather. Did we mention that rain and honeymoons are not a great mix?

AVOID POST-HONEYMOON DEBT

As with weddings, your honeymoon needs to have a budget. The honeymoon comes after a potentially expensive wedding itself, so plan accordingly. Go online and dig around for price estimates. Most airline websites will let you see the price of tickets months in advance. Factor in accommodations, leisure activities, a rental car, and other necessities. You'll want to set aside a chunk of change for food and drinks, as well. A honeymoon that involves quality accommodations and a flight will likely cost upwards of $3,000. You only get one shot at the honeymoon if all goes well, so spend a bit more than what you might be used to. You're not going to regret the vacation diet you may have to go on after the honeymoon, but you might regret a less-than-amazing honeymoon.

TIPS FOR THE SMART GROOM

If you can't afford a "proper" honeymoon, there is no shame in putting it off until your financial situation improves, so long as you do *something* within one year of your wedding—you need to celebrate, somehow! And if people ask, tell them that you're waiting until the weather gets cold or you can get more time off work.

HOW LONG CAN YOU MAKE IT LAST?

Easy does it, captain. While you might want to get away for a month, we suggest capping your honeymoon at two weeks. That's just enough time for newlyweds to avoid getting on each other's nerves. In fact, make sure you schedule some "me" time for your wife, even though we're sure you're a great guy. Send her to a spa for a couple of hours while you hit the driving range. Every man needs more practice with his five iron, and a short break from his glorious bride. This is especially true if you've never really traveled with your new wife.

What to Do When You're There

Before putting the deposit down on the hotel or paying for it up front, you should make a comprehensive list of activities for the candidate destinations. Even the heartiest of beach-goers may tire of the beach after a few days, so you'll ideally have a destination with all sorts of activities within reach.

Are you planning to bring books to read? Is there enough snorkeling to go around? What's the restaurant scene like? Consult guidebooks and message boards. You won't need to plan the honeymoon hour by hour, but you should have a sense when museums and restaurants are closed, whether festivals are starting or ending, or if your destination's must see spot has limited hours of operation. And don't forget, you're planning a honeymoon for the two of you, not just for you. It's no sweat to bring your golf clubs, but does she have a set so that she can play the round with you? Is that even something she wants to do? Have you thought about taking this opportunity to patiently teach your fiancée some of the finer points of golf rather than to improve your handicap?

The most important honeymoon activity that a groom can plan for his wife is a day at the spa. By searching on the Internet, you will be able to figure out in advance what spa facilities are around, and possibly even purchase a package in advance. You may not know the difference between a facial and a pedicure, but your wife does, and she'll be really pleased at your forethought.

TICKETS, PASSPORTS, VISAS, AND OTHER LOGISTICS

U.S. citizens can visit the State Department's website for more information on getting a passport. The point is to get your passports early. It takes as long as six weeks for processing of the passport application, and you should avoid common mistakes (like smiling!) with your passport photo. Peak periods for domestic passport processing is between January and July. That's because people are planning summer travel.

Your new wife will get a passport with your last name (if she's changing her name) *after* the wedding. Book your travel tickets in her maiden name to avoid any issues, or bring a copy of your marriage certificate.

Initiate Your Escape—Making Reservations

At this point, you should start making reservations. Booking this far in advance increases your chances of getting the various tickets you want. It also gives you more leverage if plans change later on. Some destinations may require you to send in deposits before you get a reservation.

Medical insurance is helpful if you are traveling outside of North America. While you may have medical insurance through your place of employment, the insurance rates are affordable and extra insurance is extra protection. In particular, you'll want evacuation insurance in the event that you need to get back home because of a medical emergency. This type of insurance covers emergency airlift and air travel on specialized aircraft.

LET THE COUNTDOWN BEGIN

You should do a little detective work and see if your destination will accept your debit and credit cards. More and more remote locations accept credit and debit cards every day, but you don't want to get to your destination with a wallet full of useless plastic. Furthermore, traveler's checks may not be easy to cash in some destinations. If you're honeymooning in North America, Europe, or much of the Caribbean, your credit cards will serve you well. Call your credit card issuer in advance to let them know where you're going. They'll put a note in your file.

Approaching Fast: One Month Before the Honeymoon

With one month to go before the wedding and honeymoon, everything should be in order. It's not a bad idea to reconfirm all of your reservations. Also, consider what you are leaving behind when you are gone. Do you have pets or plants? Unless they're coming with you, ask someone to take care of them. Whether it's a kennel, a petsitter, or just a nearby friend or neighbor, someone needs to be in charge of keeping all the little living things in your life happy and healthy while you're away. Put a stop to the newspaper delivery or have someone pick it up for you on a daily basis. Mail carriers won't deliver to an overflowing box, you don't want to signal to burglars that you aren't around, and you want to receive your guests' congratulatory wedding cards safely. It would be really unfortunate not to be able to enjoy all the wedding gifts you received because someone burgled your house while you were away.

Make two sets of photocopies of your itinerary, passports, credit cards (front and back), insurance, traveler's check numbers, and travel confirmation numbers. Leave one set of copies with friends or family, and slip another set of copies in your luggage.

Take a trip to the local pharmacy and refill any prescriptions and over-the-counter medications you may need. Stock up on sunblock, contact lens solution, toiletries, and anything you might not be able to find at a moment's notice on your getaway.

You're Getting Close! One Week Before the Honeymoon

Congratulations! If you've followed this guide to this point then it's time to get packing! Last-minute packing will increase the stress and decrease the excitement of travel. In addition to a big trip, you've got a wedding to worry about (and a wedding speech, remember?). Have your bags set out a couple of days before the commotion begins. Once your guests arrive in town for the wedding, there isn't going to be time to run around getting travel medical insurance. Be sure to check with the airline to see if there are any changes to restrictions on what you can and cannot bring on the plane. If you're going to be taking off on your honeymoon right after the wedding, make arrangements for someone to return your tuxedo. Ever heard of the best man? He probably has to return his own tuxedo, and it'll be no sweat for him to return yours. Your last job for this point is a simple one: Plan how you will get to the airport and how you're getting home on the return.

TIPS FOR THE SMART GROOM

Double-Check Checklist:

- Clothes for any type of weather conditions you might encounter
- Travel documents
- Photocopies of your important information
- Toiletries
- Medication
- Contacts/glasses and their appropriate cases
- Sunscreen
- Identification
- Tickets
- Traveler's checks
- Overwhelming sense of relief that the day is actually here

ten

A Bachelor Party Roadmap

SO FAR WE'VE done everything in our power to make you a smart groom. Your goal is to exceed your bride's expectations (and win rookie-of-the-year honors); we want to help you fit into the uniform. But not everything in a wedding is all about the missus ... what about you, you ask ... what about the bachelor party? Yeehaw!

A RITE OF PASSAGE

Remember when you climbed a traffic signal in college? Or when you and the boys threw eggs at a passing bus in drunken merriment? A thousand crazy nights of partying are about culminate in one memorable event. It is, of course, your bachelor party. Whether the thought of a weekend in Vegas makes you shake with delight at the prospect of paying for your wedding from the poker tables or cringe at the thought your buddies want to visit strip club after strip club, this chapter is for you.

When you commit to marrying a woman, there is a danger that you might neglect your college, high school, and work friends. It's natural, really. The person who is your best friend transitions quickly from your college roommate to your girlfriend. Friday night with the boys? Heck, you've said "pass" so many times that they might not even call you anymore!

That's part of the reason that a friend-centric ritual exists in the intervening period between your engagement and the wedding. The bachelor party is prime bonding time for you, your guy friends, your family members, and (gasp!) your future in-laws. Despite the lore of the bachelor party involving erotic dancers and copious amounts of alcohol, the modern bachelor party appears to be shedding much of the X-rated content. Indeed, many bachelor parties these days are mild bachelor parties, rather than wild bachelor parties. We'll cover both styles, just in case.

WHO'S IN CHARGE OF PARTY PLANNING?

The best man is usually in charge of organizing the bachelor party. In some cases, a male sibling or groomsman is a more appropriate choice, depending on experience with planning and suitability as a master of fun and partying. Needless to say, whoever is in charge has to have a track record of competence. The bulk of the organizing will be placed on his able shoulders. Aside from putting the whole shindig together, the organizer is responsible for ensuring that you have a great time, but don't do anything that will jeopardize your impending nuptials. (This really does happen from time to time, and makes for great reading in the newspapers.)

With the goal of staying out of the papers and your fiancée's doghouse, you need to be able to trust the organizer to respect the tone you've set for the event. This person should make everyone feel included. He must endeavor to maximize enjoyment and minimize discomfort for you and the guests. It's a tough job. He should have the enthusiasm and style to pull it off. Choose wisely.

When to Schedule the Celebration

It could be during the summer or spring or on a freezing winter day in February. But under no circumstances should you allow your bachelor party to be held the night before the wedding ceremony. We suspect that your bride, her family, your friends, and your Grandma Nelly will be extremely upset if you show up intoxicated or incoherent or need to take a minute to "puke" in the middle of the wedding ceremony. Green-faced grooms don't make perfect photo subjects, and perfect photos are what your bride expects of you.

TIPS FOR THE SMART GROOM

Your fiancée and soon-to-be wife may feel that the bachelor party is a knock on the marriage itself. She probably does not want to know what goes on, let alone think about it. Have a chat with your bride-to-be, and put her in touch with your organizer early on. A frank discussion with your fiancée about the bachelor party sends the message that communication is important to you and that you want to avoid any potential issues that may arise. You'll get a good sense of whether she can handle some shenanigans or would prefer that you guys just stuck to the golf course or go-karts.

That said, the timing of the bachelor party can be difficult, as you may want to schedule the party so that your guests who are traveling from afar can attend both your bachelor party and your wedding using only one return trip. Accordingly, the typical bachelor party is held two to three months in advance of a wedding or on the Thursday night prior to a Saturday wedding, for example.

IF YOU CHOOSE A MILD BACHELOR PARTY . . .

Long before the bachelor party, you and the organizer need to set the tone of the bachelor party.

Defining the tone in advance is important since it will not be possible to do so on the night of the party, despite your or your organizer's best attempts. Setting the tone will also help guests get a heads-up in terms of what to expect. This can be useful, particularly if some of your guests are expecting a wild party or have never considered that a great bachelor party doesn't always involve lots of booze and strippers. Once the tone is set, the details are traditionally kept from you. It's a surprise. Deal with it.

A mild bachelor party could involve:
- A house party
- Classy cigars and rum tasting
- A poker tournament
- Attending a sports event
- A golf outing (with lessons and time at the driving range)
- A skiing trip
- Go-kart racing
- Paintball
- A bonfire in the backyard
- A steak dinner

Picture it: Even your most conservative friends are going to have a *great* time with paintball followed by a steak dinner. A mild bachelor party involves no risk and may just be more fun than a wild bachelor party. But, if you're more inclined to living on the wild side . . .

ROCKIN' WITH THE WILD BACHELOR PARTY

If you're more open to a "last chance for fun," a wild bachelor party is for you. Whether you have your party in San Juan, Las Vegas, Montreal, your hometown, or any dozen spots in between, wild bachelor parties are part of the lore of transitioning from bachelorhood to married man. By "wild" bachelor party, we generally mean one that involves copious amounts of alcohol, gambling, exotic dancers, mingling with bachelorette parties that are also taking place, and white, stretch Hummer SUVs. It's not exactly for the faint of heart or the pious. Many guys would expect nothing less.

That said, it's still not a bad idea to get your fiancée's blessing. She's no dummy and will expect that if you're headed to a destination bachelor party, strippers might be involved. If you don't feel like having such a conversation with your fiancée, make sure that you put her in touch with your bachelor party organizer. Obviously, if you have your own reservations about the tone, you need to be clear on your limits with the organizer, who can then crack with whip with your attendees.

So What Exactly Is the Difference Between Mild and Wild?

Both the mild bachelor party and wild bachelor party can start the same way. Make a day of it with a golf tournament, a steak dinner, and a poker night. There can be a gradual progression of the day's events. Things will start to be different after dinner—either your guests will pack up and go home, or hop in a limo and head out to the clubs.

Get a Room—For Yourself!

Whether the wild bachelor party is staged somewhere exotic or in your hometown, we suggest that you not return to your actual home after the late partying. Spend an extra $150 and get a hotel room or stay with a buddy. The next morning you can convalesce on your own and not disturb your fiancée, who will invariably ask "So, how was it?" (Read: "You didn't do anything stupid, right?")

The Destination Bachelor Party

Far-fetched? Not really. One best man arranged a fifteen-man trip to Montreal from New York for a weekend-long bachelor party. Best of all, he did it while keeping the groom completely in the dark. The groom was literally kidnapped from his place of work on a Friday afternoon. He had no idea where he was going, let alone out of the country, until they got to the airport. The clever best man was in cahoots with the bride-to-be, who had slipped him the groom's passport and gave her blessing to the trip, along with plenty of ground rules. Details such as proper travel documents and arranging all transportation well ahead of time is what makes a destination-hopping bachelor party work. If the organizer comes up with something like this, then you will be a legend in the making. Just make sure that you can trust the person organizing the event.

Destination Party Ideas:
- Las Vegas (bachelor party capital of the world)
- Montreal (a close second, something different and comparatively inexpensive)
- New York (no shortage of partying venues)
- New Orleans (New Orleans is open for business)
- Amsterdam (dangerous, but lots of fun)

WHO GETS AN INVITE?

You should outline the number of guests you want to attend your bachelor party. Your organizer may only know a few of your friends, so it will be helpful for him to have a list of names and e-mail addresses. How many people can attend depends on how many friends you have and where they live, the kind of bachelor party you want, and how many people the activities can accommodate. Fifteen is an ideal number; any more than that, and things will be difficult to control as the day or night goes on.

One of the easiest ways to coordinate the bachelor party is with an e-mail invitation, or e-vite. That way, the organizer can let everyone know what's on the party agenda, including key contact information dates, and meeting points.

THE DAY OF THE BASH

When the day of the party arrives, you should ensure your organizer has a list of guests, as he certainly will not know all of your friends. He should give the guests his cell phone number, especially those guests arriving from out of town. Flights get cancelled or delayed and people get lost, so it's key to have a reliable means of contact.

Transportation

If the organizer has planned the party properly, there will be some form of transportation involved, be it your legs or a stretch limo. With a manageable number of attendees, a limousine is not out of the question and provides a safe way for the group to get around.

A Ticketed Bachelor Party

No matter where your bachelor party takes place, you've got to keep in mind that not all the attendees will be able to drop cash on bottle service if they've forked over money to an airline just to attend. The same goes for dinner and whatever else your best man has got planned. If he's a spendthrift, don't expect everyone else to be. A good way to cover the costs associated with the bachelor party is to sell tickets to the guests. Not only does this help pay for the event, but it also gives the guests an idea of what they can expect to spend for the evening or weekend. The price of the ticket should pay for some activities (such as a round of golf or admission to a club) and a meal. Guests should be responsible for covering the cost of their own drinks.

HAVE FUN!

The best part of planning a bachelor party is that the groom is kept in the dark about some of it. Once you and the organizer have laid out the ground rules for the night, the organizer will feel free to plan some surprises within that framework. Did you forget to mention that under no circumstances would you dress in drag or beg for kisses on the cheek from local ladies? Too bad for you!

Be ready to dive in and roll with any surprises that might come your way. Grooms need to be good sports. A good bachelor party is as much a roast of the groom as a celebration with friends.

Rules about Speaking of, about, and to the Bride

Nothing will ruin a wild bachelor party like a loose-lipped friend blabbing all about it to his girl-friend who just happens to be your fiancée's best friend. What happens at a bachelor party (be it mild or wild) should stay etched in memory alone. It's an unspoken rule, but your organizer should state this rule explicitly to your trusted guests. No cameras or camera phones. What happens on this bachelor party can never be spoken about. It builds a sense of brotherhood and secrecy, which we guys inherently love. Have fun!

eleven

Practice Makes Perfect: Toasts, Speeches, the Rehearsal, and the Rehearsal Dinner

IT'S A VERY good idea not to fall flat on your face when it comes to making a wedding toast or speech. Practice really does make perfect. Not only will you practice your wedding speech, but you're likely to practice the wedding itself, in the form of the wedding rehearsal and rehearsal dinner. Guess who typically plans and pays for the rehearsal dinner?

WEDDING TOASTS AND SPEECHES

Nowadays, there is much confusion about who toasts whom and when, and especially whether uninvited toastmasters can get up and spin a yarn about your ex-girlfriends. It may not surprise you to learn there are no hard-and-fast rules anymore, but that doesn't mean you should ignore tradition altogether. The standard order for wedding toasts is as follows:

- Father of the bride, toasting his daughter
- The groom, toasting his bride
- The best man, toasting the newlyweds

You may never have attended a wedding that went in this order, and for good reason: It is slightly counterintuitive. No one says a thing about you, for instance, and your family seems strangely absent from the proceedings. You may also notice no female ever lifts a glass. Accordingly, toasts are done in whatever order people wish, according to their own logic. Typically, however, the father of the bride makes the first speech and toast, as he is traditionally paying for the reception. Of course, many a father of the bride nowadays is *not* paying for the reception and may not necessarily need to open it.

HOW TO MAKE A PROPER WEDDING SPEECH

Wedding speeches will be a central part of your reception. A good speech needs to be original. You won't be able to deliver the speech effectively if it has been taken from a cookie-cutter, fill-in-the-blank speech you found online or from a book (like this one!). These speeches never reflect who you are. The worst part is the audience will know that you didn't write that speech or any of the jokes you delivered. With that in mind, this survival guide will give you the tools you need to write and present a good speech, cover some do's and don'ts, and provide all-important instructions on how to fight nerves. We don't expect you to be a writer of prose, but we do expect that you try to be the kind of groom we'd be proud of.

GroomGroove.com's Speech Rules

At a minimum, your speech should be two minutes in length. It may be the longest two minutes of your life. Believe it or not, these minutes will go by very quickly, especially if you have followed the advice and prepared the speech a couple weeks in advance. It's safest to follow a prepared text or bullet points rather than deliver something off-the-cuff.

Preparing the text will keep you on your game when you're delivering it and allows you to say something that is meaningful. If you foresee getting nervous, the easiest thing to do is to read from a prepared text. This technique is especially a good idea for those who are terrified of public speaking. As you're reading the text, you will want to make eye contact with your audience every few words or sentences. That means looking up from your paper to the very back of the room while speaking, and periodically making direct eye contact with individuals. The key is to look up frequently and keep speaking while doing so. Put your speech on cue cards or sheets of paper, which will allow you to print your speech and make edits easily. Number your pages to safeguard against your sheets falling off the podium. Make sure that you print your speech so that the lettering is large enough to read with ease. Finally, put the speech inside your jacket before you leave for the ceremony. ("Dammit, where did I put my speech?" is not what you want to be thinking as you slowly walk up to the mic.)

TIPS FOR THE SMART GROOM

You may have the awesome idea of an open mic throughout the wedding reception, allowing guests to come up and present a liquor-charged anecdote about you and your bride. Having witnessed a number of these performances, the guys at GroomGroove.com advise you to avoid this. For every touching anecdote from your uncle, someone will invariably get up and make a total fool of themselves or embarrass your bride.

What to Say and How to Say It

Structure your speech. Avoid rambling. You want to recognize close friends and family, many of who have traveled long distances to witness the wedding. You'll want to speak about your bride and in particular, how you met. Finally, you should take this time to express your shared values, hopes, and dreams. Don't have any material on that subject? Reread Chapter 1 of this book and get thinking.

Get to the Point, Cleverly and Easily

A good structure brings the audience along for the ride. It makes the experience more enjoyable and is the cornerstone of good writing. Structure isn't terribly difficult. An ideal wedding speech should be structured as follows:

1. Tell the audience what you're going to tell them. "Today, I want to speak about Jen. I want to tell you how we met, and why she's the best thing that's ever happened to me." (A note to the groom-to-be: Please avoid using the name "Jen" in your own wedding speech, unless that's your girl's name. That will be awkward for all.)

2. Tell the audience about Jen. Tell them how you met, and why she's the best thing that's ever happened to you.

3. Tell the audience, in one sentence, what you just told them. "And now you know how Jen and I met, and most important, why I love her."

That's called the *wham, bam speech*, and will leave your friends, family (and father-in-law) thinking you're the best thing in the world.

A Memorable Speech

Humor is an important part of a wedding speech as it puts both you and the audience at ease. The best joke is in an anecdote, because as speaker, you put the audience in your shoes, and it's genuine. People will pay attention, if, as described above, you explain how you met your wife, in your own words. Generally, your speech will never be as funny as the best man's speech. That's because he gets to roast you. You, on the other hand, will not roast your bride.

You want people either to remember your speech as heartfelt or not to remember your speech at all. At the conclusion of your speech, remember to thank the guests for attending.

HOW NOT TO CHOKE

Practice makes perfect. The most important thing you can do is to write and edit your speech a few weeks in advance, and practice the delivery. As a calming technique, you can also practice the speech in the room where it will be delivered.

Timing is everything. Ask the MC when exactly your speech will be so that you can mentally prepare. You don't want to be surprised. Take a few slow deep breaths before the MC calls you up; as you are getting up from your seat and before you begin, say "Good afternoon." Rhythmic breathing will force your heart to slow down. Go slowly at first and pause between your first few sentences. People often think they are speaking slowly when in fact they are not.

It's Okay to Be Nervous

Admitting to your audience that you are nervous can calm you down, because your audience will crack a laugh with you. When they laugh, you relax. Remember, the audience is there for the wedding and not to critique your speechmaking ability. Did we mention preparation? Yeah, that helps too.

THE PURPOSE OF THE WEDDING REHEARSAL

"So, where do I walk to?" Most organized wedding ceremonies will have scheduled a mock ceremony the evening before wedding day. Having a run through is extremely important to avoid any creeping nervousness about the wedding ceremony experience itself, as we suspect there will other things to be nervous about. The venue may provide a wedding coordinator, or perhaps the officiant himself will instruct members of the wedding party and anyone who has any kind of role in the ceremony about what they need to do.

TIPS FOR THE SMART GROOM

The rehearsal dinner is a time to bring your entire wedding party, your parents, and your future-in-laws together for a relaxing evening before the big day. Not only is it an opportunity to thank them for all their support throughout the wedding planning process, but it's also a great way to unwind. That said, it is often better to organize a low-key, casual dinner where guests can sit around in jeans and T-shirts than to plan something formal. If you decide to have a more casual affair, you can order pizza or sandwiches, or organize a potluck. The objective is to keep things comfortable for the guests, to reduce costs, and to make the affair as easy to organize as possible. You will have enough stress as it is.

While it's pretty easy to follow instructions, inevitably someone will show up late to the rehearsal or not be able to make it at all. That's where your best man comes in. The people that need to show at the rehearsal include the best man, groomsmen, ushers, ring bearers, flower girls, the maid of honor, the bridesmaids, anyone reading or singing during the ceremony, the officiant (probably), and of course, you and the bride. You'll work through pacing, positioning, and expectations during this shortened version of the actual ceremony. (The rehearsal, by the way, is a convenient opportunity to deal with any fees you need to pay to the person performing your wedding.)

In the event the actual venue is not available, you should consider hosting a mock ceremony at the hotel or in a living room.

YOUR WEDDING VOWS

If you're the type that detested writing assignments in school, then the vow that your officiant chooses and you repeat aloud is your best bet. But if you believe in being different or mildly creative, or you don't want to speak someone else's words at your wedding, then the personalized vow will work for you.

In your personal vow, you'll want to focus on the qualities that drew you to your bride and any memories that can be tied into the general theme of the vow. Keep in mind that your bride will also have to prepare a similar statement, as it'll be slightly awkward if you prepare something elaborate but she just recites standard vows. You may even opt to work on these vows together.

If you decide to keep the vows a surprise for the special day, you may want to consider running them by a friend just to be on the safe side. Personalized vows may require more time and effort, but in the end, the reward will be in the eyes of your bride.

When the Time Comes to Speak

What about jitters? You're going to be Nervous Nelly on your wedding day. If there's any way that you're likely to stumble and forget your personalized vows, it will be awkward for everyone involved. While it is out of the ordinary to write your vows on a small cue card, it may be a good idea if you are truly in a bind and are worried about forgetting the words for this all-important minute. Under no circumstances will you write the vows on your hand. You're not cheating on a high school test here.

Whether you craft your own vows or go with the "repeat after me" method, say your vows slowly and enunciate. Look into your bride's eyes when you say them. While the marriage certificate is signed by the couple after the ceremony, the marriage contract really gets signed by the eyes.

twelve

Wedding Week
(and More Gifts to Buy)

IN THIS CHAPTER, we'll try to paint a picture of how your wedding week and day will actually go. The day will feel a bit like a whirlwind, but by reading this chapter, you'll have an idea what to expect in a traditional wedding on Saturday afternoon. Your wedding, of course, might be very different. In addition, we'll also cover the gifts you may want to purchase for your best man, groomsmen, and possibly even your bride.

WEDDING WEEK ITINERARY

There's no doubt that your wedding is going to be different in some ways from every other Joe getting married (and there are 44,000 Joes getting married—every single weekend), but for the sake of letting you know what to expect, here is a wedding day itinerary so that you can avoid saying "maybe I forgot something" hundreds of times.

The Day Before—Relax for the Rehearsal and Rehearsal Dinner

Whatever the season, you should attempt to relax on the day before the wedding. Your guests will have begun to arrive in the days prior to the wedding, and a whole flood of people will show up the day before. Guess whom they're looking to talk to? This is a chance to catch up with friends and family whom you haven't seen in a long time. You will already have picked up your wedding attire from the tuxedo rental shop, tried it on, and taken care of any last-minute issues. Smile, shake hands, give lots of hugs, and be merry. This is your time to impress—particularly with *her* family and friends who are doubtlessly wondering if you're a schmuck or a good guy.

The Wedding Rehearsal

The wedding rehearsal is a mock ceremony that takes place in the early afternoon or evening on the day before the wedding. It will help you, your bride, your families, and other players calm their nerves. The rehearsal will answer questions such as when to sit down, when to stand up, and when to say "I do." Importantly, you'll learn where exactly you're going to be holed up, nervously awaiting your glorious bride's arrival. If you have any questions about any part of the ceremony, now's the time to speak up.

The Rehearsal Dinner

This can be as informal as sandwiches or as formal as a sit-down meal at an expensive restaurant requiring reservations and some advanced planning. As the groom's family is traditionally the host of the rehearsal dinner, this is your chance to shine. Go easy on the wine, and try to call it a night early. You'll sleep alone the night before your wedding. Tradition holds that you are not to see your bride until the morning of the wedding when she arrives at the ceremony.

THE DAY OF THE WEDDING

Hopefully well rested, you will kick off the day with a hearty and healthy breakfast with your best man and the groomsmen. Keep the conversation light and talk about the Yankees or the great honeymoon you've got planned. Wear jeans and a T-shirt. Smile, even if you're nervous. (And you're going to be.)

Get Dressed (Tuxedo Time!)—
Only about an Hour of Bachelorhood Left

After breakfast, you'll want to get dressed in your tuxedo, suit, beach gear, or whatever it is that you're wearing for wedding day. Shave, shower, and put on your best face. It's probably helpful to have your attendants meet you where you are staying, be it at a hotel room or at home, to get ready together. Why? Typically, boutonnieres will be delivered to the groom on the morning of the wedding. Furthermore, you'll be able to control the whereabouts of your part of the wedding party. Many couples will document the wedding day by having the groom and his attendants pose for photos with their photographer as they are getting ready, or once they are ready.

Pre-Ceremony—
Thirty to Forty-Five Minutes to Go

You'll have arrived at the wedding ceremony thirty to forty minutes prior to the ceremony. You'll want to use this time to remain sane and entertained with the help of your groomsmen and best man. You should greet as many people as you can as they enter the ceremony venue. That said, if you're feeling nervous, go to the staging area and relax.

The Ceremony Itself—
About Thirty Minutes

"*Thirty minutes?!*" Yes, all this wedding planning culminates in less than forty-five minutes of actual wedding (and often fewer). It's also the most important part—don't be fooled.

Hopefully you remembered when and where to stand or sit and the general order of proceedings. You probably won't believe this moment has arrived. Take in all that you see. Savor this classic moment, as you'll remember it for your lifetime, even if it starts to become a bit of a blur.

Post-Ceremony—
About an Hour

Between the ceremony and the grand entrance of the newlyweds at their wedding reception, the wedding party will step away from the watchful eyes of the guests to have additional wedding photos taken with their photographer. This could be at a location near the ceremony itself, or the couple may have planned to hop in a Batmobile to a special place designated for this purpose. All of your pent-up nervousness will have dissipated. You are married now. Congratulations!

THE RECEPTION—
ABOUT THREE HOURS

Food, drink, and speeches. That's about all you
should worry about. Make sure both you and your
wedding MC know when your speech or toast takes
place. Don't be caught off-guard, as that will add
significantly to your nervousness when you are
called upon. Remember to visit each table after the
meal to chat with your guests and thank them for
coming. You'll cut the wedding cake and the party
will begin. Cue the music and dancing.

TIPS FOR THE SMART GROOM

You may be asked to do the first dance. Count-
less local dance halls and private instructors
offer dance lessons throughout the year. Most of
these do wedding packages as well, ensuring you
always have a swing, fox trot, or waltz in your tool
bag should the need arise. Dance lessons can be
fun and therapeutic, and you can avoid the kind
of spectacular falls that might otherwise land you
on YouTube (and not in a good way). You may also
take comfort in the fact that there is infinitely more
leeway these days when it comes to your first
dance. A growing number of couples are bucking
tradition altogether, largely because they simply
cannot dance!

An Alcohol-Free Wedding . . .

An open bar or cash bar wedding is a great occasion with the right crowd. Having liquor flowing with a bartender serving up beverages can be fun, easy, and bring out great . . . spirit. That said, an alcohol-free wedding may be preferable if you want to avoid any issues, are in a cash crunch, or don't actually drink in the first place. You should not feel obliged to have booze at your wedding. And as for toasts, nonalcoholic champagne is equally festive and bubbly. You can also substitute alcohol with a coffee bar serving up espresso, cappuccino, and mochas. You're going to face a bit of ribbing from your beer-drinking college friends, so you may wish to float the concept to them long before the wedding and the reception.

The Escape—Around Midnight

While friends and family are having a blast at the reception, the bride and groom typically make their escape at around midnight for some well-deserved rest. You'll see everyone in the morning.

WEDDING NIGHT PERFORMANCE

Sex on your wedding night carries ambiguous expectations; as you walk back to your hotel room, you will feel a combination of exhilaration and exhaustion. Ultimately, only one of these competing sensations will win. Much of the drama surrounding wedding night sex is lore, handed down by generations claiming to abstain until matrimony. It may be unlikely that your wedding night will involve a pair of clumsy virgins cutting through the palpable nervous energy.

You may find yourself struggling to perform, or even forcing yourself to get in the mood. Don't worry; the beautiful lady on the other side of the veil will be thinking the same thing. Common sense should win the day.

If you and your wife are not in the mood, don't go through the motions for the sake of form. After all, you're likely to have spent a pretty exhausting day greeting both sides of your families, friends, and people you don't really know well. To start a lifetime of marital sex with "Oh, let's get this over with" contradicts everything else that the day stands for. If you have the energy and the inclination, enjoy your first night as a husband. You are ready. Your wife is ready. You know what comes next. But if you're too tired, wait until your plane touches down at the honeymoon destination. Once you get to the hotel, we mean.

(ANOTHER) GIFT FOR YOUR FIANCÉE

Gifts are part of the wedding story, be it the engagement ring or gifts for your best man and groomsmen. You may not know that it is becoming customary to give your new wife a congratulatory gift to commemorate the marriage. It's not an official requirement, so feel free to skip it. That said, if you're into thanking your bride, the gift should be long-lasting, sentimental, and have some symbolic personal value. It also needs to be something she is unlikely to receive from one of the guests. Jewelry is an obvious choice, but perhaps you can do something more personal or interesting. For example, if your fiancée is a brainiac and loves to read, you could purchase all of the Pulitzer Prize fiction winners for a certain period. If that's too brainy for your taste, we do know that no woman will turn down a day at the spa. The point is that while a gift from the groom to the bride is not mandatory, it is a nice touch and need not break the bank. Give your bride this gift after the wedding, but before the honeymoon.

THANK-YOU GIFTS FOR YOUR GROOMSMEN

While you've been busy helping your fiancée pick out invitations and seating charts, your best man and groomsmen have been getting fitted for tuxedos, preparing and practicing toasts, and planning a wild bachelor party for you (free-of-charge for you). To show the boys how much you appreciate their friendship, it's customary to give each of them a gift. You should spend anywhere from $50 to $100 per groomsman. Avoid buying anything too cheap, as this gift should also be a long-lasting and memorable item.

The gift for your best man could be more substantial. This is one time to really thank him for being there over the years. Plan to purchase a gift for him in the $75 to $150 range. Here are some gift suggestions for the groomsmen and best man:

- Box of cigars
- Zippo lighters
- Engraved money clip
- Flask or beer stein
- Sports-related equipment
- Gadgets or toys
- Executive pen
- Pocketknife
- Desk caddy
- Toolbox

But Are They Going to Use It?

Giving a gift that gets used is always better than giving one that ends up sitting in a drawer. A popular idea is to buy a clothing accessory that matches the tuxedo the groomsmen will wear at the wedding. Cufflinks are an easy option. A wristwatch allows you to avoid engravings and makes sure he arrives at your wedding on time. A quality dress shirt for the rented tuxedos is a good option. (There is no reason to wear the hyperstarched and 20 percent cotton shirt that is provided in the package.)

It may be easier to get something involving food, beer, or sports, such as the following gifts:

- Barbecue kit
- Beer-of-the-Month subscription
- Engraved cork/bottle-opener
- An expensive bottle of red wine or rum
- Steaks delivered to the front door
- Steak brander
- Golf gear
- Tickets to a game

Surprise Them—Shake Up Tradition

Thinking outside of the box is a surefire way of showing your groomsmen how much you appreciate them. You can easily surprise them with some of these ideas:

- Shares of stock in a company (for example, Harley-Davidson)
- Shaving kit for travel
- MP3 player

Giving a gift tailored to their hobbies or interests is a great way to ensure success. If your groomsmen all have different personalities, don't feel like you have to give everyone the same gift. As long as you stay in the same price range, no one should feel ripped off or jealous. Put thought into these gifts and make them personal because, after all, these are your buddies, and you should have a happy group of groomsmen come wedding day.

WHAT IF IT'S NOT YOUR FIRST WEDDING?

A second (or third) wedding will still be a great event for you. It can also be a sensitive time for the new bride if she has never been married. Add children from the past marriage to the mix, and the second wedding—let alone the third marriage—may test your skills.

Regardless of who's getting married and whether children are involved, this new wedding should be a new day for a new beginning, with no reference to what came before. If you weren't really involved in your first wedding, perhaps you should consider setting a different tone for round two.

TIPS FOR THE SMART GROOM

A great way to keep younger children happy is to set up a "junior reception" complete with invitations to some of their friends and young relatives. You might find the children will be so excited to host their own party that they won't even care much about the "adult ceremony."

Children in the Wedding

Children from a previous marriage can play important ancillary roles such as ring bearers or flower girls. If you have slightly older children involved, a young adult can act as a junior bridesmaid or groomsman. His tuxedo or her dress should be the same as the older groomsmen or bridesmaids. The children will feel much more involved than they otherwise would. Furthermore, if you are having a religious ceremony where there will be readings, you can ask that your children take an active part.

thirteen

Overcoming Last-Minute Jitters

THAT CREEPING REALIZATION that you're making a huge commitment to one person for life may leave you in a cold sweat. Close your eyes and the feeling will soon pass. Nearly every groom has second thoughts (particularly after a nice little heated argument with his fiancée). Here's how to combat cold feet.

GETTING COLD FEET?

Last-minute emotional rushes can be overwhelming for even the most steadfast of grooms. Don't be surprised by this sudden feeling that you're headed downriver without a paddle, with a waterfall at the end. You may have a lingering feeling that you're too young or too carefree to be tied down. You may even question whether your bride is the right one for you. While men have long been accused of lacking emotional sensitivity, there's no doubt that we have emotions, and nervousness is one of them.

But now let some rational thoughts take over. You have taken these steps toward marriage because she is "The One," both on an emotional and physical level, and stands to maximize your happiness. If you had felt that this was an arrangement destined for failure, you would have known long before. Ward off nervousness by going for a run or hitting the gym. Focus on positive thoughts and think about the honeymoon, happiness, and children ("What!?") your marriage will produce. Of course, there are compelling reasons to call off a marriage, but cold feet is not one of them.

EVERYBODY GETS THE JITTERS— EVEN YOUR BRIDE

The good news is that you are in good company. It's a natural reaction for a groom to ponder whether he's making the right choice, particularly with the divorce rate being what it is. The key to solving jitters, however, is to take a big deep breath, relax, and probe what exactly is bothering you. It could be anything from the Ten Tough Questions to money issues to fear of commitment. It is, however, in your best interests to hurdle over any jitters if you're this far down the path to wedding and a marriage. Jitters, of course, vary in terms of degrees. Chances are, you probably haven't paid much attention to how you and your fiancée resolve disputes.

Honesty Can Save the Day

If you and your fiancée are solid communicators, it's okay to voice that you're a bit nervous. She may be nervous too. By talking about it, you may untie that awful knot in your stomach that won't otherwise seem to go away. If your reticence to marry is based on a few minor problems with her that you'd like to see changed in married life, you can initiate this discussion with her in a positive tone. She probably has a short wish list of constructive criticism(s) as well.

As we had previously discussed, many of the minor tremors in a relationship can be met head-on with a dose of premarital or marital counseling. Rather than being a sign of defeat, it's really a sign of courage and devotion to the institution of marriage. It's a sign of your willingness to make it work.

Seek Some Help—Call on Your Best Man

Your best man is supposed to be your confidant. He's the guy whom you should speak to if you've got cold feet. Be honest with him, and he'll give you the straight goods on whether you're being totally irrational or have a valid concern. Don't count only on your own judgment, as you're not likely to be in the best position to determine whether you're being irrational. Trust his judgment, or go to your brother, your father, or a professional therapist. Get over yourself and go speak to someone you trust.

Legitimate Doubts

If you've got very legitimate doubts about whether the person you are about to marry is the right person for you, however, you owe it to yourself and to your fiancée to think long and hard in the months before wedding day whether you should go through with it. There is a reason that most engagements last for upwards of six months, and why engagements are called off from time to time. Calling off an engagement is likely a permanent step. It will be next to impossible to go from planning a wedding and a life together back to being boyfriend and girlfriend. Breaking off an engagement is not easy, but it may be a wise and courageous decision. Canceling an engagement is not shameful, and your fiancée will eventually be grateful after calling it off, having avoided becoming Mrs. Ex-You.

There are some valid reasons to call off your wedding. Here are some examples:

- You still have strong feelings for an ex-girl-friend, or you know you are marrying the wrong person.
- You are marrying her because it seems like the "right thing to do."
- You have vastly and insurmountable divergent views on the Ten Tough Questions.
- One of you has a major issue with trust.
- An important promise is broken.
- You are not capable of being faithful and selfless.

These are some of the primary indicators for increasing divorce rates. As the offspring of the "divorce generation" begin to reach marrying age, they're realizing that they would rather be disengaged than divorced.

And in case you were wondering, if the engagement is called off, it is customary for the bride to return the engagement ring to the groom. It also must be awkward.

THE PROPER WAY TO CALL IT OFF

Not showing up for your wedding just doesn't happen, and it certainly would not happen to a guy reading this book! That being said, there is a proper way to call off an engagement or a wedding—if you really have to do it.

First, you must inform the principal players in a timely fashion. Of course, you should explain to your fiancée why you have made this decision. Be resolute about your choice. You want to call it off within a reasonable amount of time before the wedding. The longer you wait, the more painful calling it off will become. There is no easy way to go about closing the wedding-planning process without having a wedding.

What about the Gifts, Ring, and Other Expenses?

If you've resolved that calling off your engagement is the best and only decision, questions about funds, rings, and gifts returned or kept will inevitably come up. As a rule, gifts given to you as a result of peoples' expectation should be returned to the giver. This includes gifts of money, which hopefully have not already been spent.

You will need to contact any companies or individual whose services were organized in conjunction with your wedding, including everyone from tuxedo rental houses, photographers, officiants, reception halls, ceremony locations, travel agencies, hotels, car rental companies, and caterers, to name a few. Most will have cancellation policies. If a formal engagement announcement has already gone out to the guests, then a subsequent, revised announcement, such as the following, should be sent as soon as possible:

"Mr. and Mrs. John Doe regret to inform the community/the guests that their son/daughter will no longer be marrying Jane/Dick Smith."

There is absolutely no obligation to explain to the invitees why your engagement was broken—it simply is not their business. If people are morbidly curious, you should be as diplomatic and brief as possible. The awkwardness will pass soon after this is all over, but not if you attack your ex-fiancée, cursing her for all her shortcomings. Be shrewd. Although backing out is a major decision and not without consequences, it is the wisest, more gracious thing to do when your feelings toward marrying this person drastically change. You may not get a round of applause, but it is far braver than going through with marriage when you know the marriage will not succeed.

fourteen

The Happily-Ever-After Part

THE HONEYMOON IS over, so to speak, and you and your bride are no longer the center of attention. But other than writing and sending out thank-you cards, you're on your own with your wife and your life. We wish the very best of luck to you.

EASY THANK-YOU CARDS

You and your new wife have returned from the honeymoon. The wedding was a success, everything turned out just the way you had planned it. You have one last duty to perform—sending out meaningful wedding thank-you cards. While you may believe you can sneak away to watch the football game, that isn't the way this will work; you're going to write personal messages to your grandmother, college buddies, her friends and your friends, and your families. By the way: it is perfectly acceptable to write your thank-you cards while watching Monday night football.

Before you tackle this task, make sure that you are up to speed on thank-you card etiquette. There are two essential points you need to know:

1. You must send a card to everyone who gave you a gift. You should have a list of gifts you received and from whom. This includes
    - Your guests;
    - Anyone who did not attend your wedding, but who sent you a gift;
    - Anyone who provided a service as their gift (baked the wedding cake, lent you a car); and
    - Everyone in your wedding party, including your parents and in-laws.

2. Thank-you cards should be sent promptly, within two to four weeks after the wedding. Any later than one month is a faux pas. All cards must be personal and handwritten in either blue or black ink. Although we are now living in an age of technology where e-mail has become a perfectly acceptable way to send invitations, greeting cards, birthday cards, and even RSVPs, it is not good form to send your thanks via e-mail.

Ideally, you'll write proper and well-mannered thank-you notes that allow your personality and sincerity to come through. Write from the heart, in your own words. Write about how you'll use the gift. Write about how much you appreciated that your guests attended the wedding, and how you're looking forward to married life. Write the words repeatedly until you are through.

TIPS FOR THE SMART GROOM

Yes, the rumors are true. Your guests have up to one year to send you a wedding gift. Now, the truth is, you'll receive most gifts on your wedding day or even a bit afterwards. Where gifts are not sent, however, it is likely that they were not properly delivered from the store where your gift registry is kept or perhaps a card was lost in the mail. After a few months, there is no harm in checking in with your guests. As the groom, you should ensure that a table is set up for receiving gifts, and create a box with a slot for people to put greeting cards. A folding table with a white linen table cloth is ideal.

A Cheat Sheet for Thank-You Cards

You're lucky. We've been there and know that writing thank-you cards is somewhat painful. Here's a cheat sheet:

Dear [insert name],

Thank you for being part of our wedding day with us and for your thoughtful gift. The [insert gift] will be a perfect fit for in our [choose: kitchen, living room, dining room, bedroom, bathroom]. Again, thank you for your kindness and your blessings, and for thinking of us on our wedding day.

Your friends, [insert your names]

Of course, we don't advocate taking the above attempt at thank-you cards as gospel. Create something unique for yourself. What would you say to the recipient if they were in front of you, in no fewer than three sentences?

MOVING IN

You may have cohabitated with your new wife before getting married. If so, both of you will be intimately familiar with each other's routine and habits. If you've read the Ten Tough Questions at the outset of this book, however, you'll have had a frank discussion about the kind of things that may bother you and your spouse. If you haven't had such a conversation, it's a very good idea.

You may never have realized that your penchant for leaving breakfast dishes on the coffee table (even if it's only while you shower) drives your wife insane. You may never have expressed to your wife that you'd prefer she not file her nails while sitting on the couch with you.

These may seem like minor annoyances, but even minor annoyances can build into major distractions, particularly if they act as a screen for deeper marital issues. If she expresses annoyance with your breakfast dishes, it is very possible she's really concerned about a larger issue, such as finances, your time with friends, or intimacy.

It can also be helpful to develop a routine with your spouse for home tasks. Who is responsible for shoveling the driveway, washing dishes, or taking out the garbage, and when?

Even if the transition to a marital home will be easy (or if you're already living together), you should try to make a significant change to make your new abode a marital home. This woman, after all, is your wife, not your old roommate.

BEGINNING THE REST OF YOUR LIVES TOGETHER

Good riddance to wedding planning. On to the tough stuff. We know that approximately 52 percent of the time, this marriage of yours is going to last till death do you part. We hope you're on the successful side of 52 percent.

The only way you can stay on the positive side of the divorce statistics is by putting real effort into your relationship, and, in particular, into fostering open communication. Marriage is hard work. It is infinitely harder than being fitted for a tuxedo. We sincerely believe that it is not a sign of defeat to visit a marriage counselor from time to time, even if you perceive that things are just peachy. Over time, married couples tend to adapt to the stressors of living together or raising a family. Rather than just "putting up" with your spouse, or having her put up with you, recognize that the marriage is really the biggest investment of your life. If something is bothering you, say so. If you think something is bothering your wife, ask. Recognize the potential fault lines before they develop into deep chasms.

Plan Now or Forever Hold Your Peace

You've put some effort into planning and executing your wedding. This rite of passage is really a sign of your commitment to your new life with your new wife. All of the pomp and circumstance of weddings pales in comparison to what lies ahead.

Thank you for reading this book. And good luck. You won the rookie-of-the-year award. Check out GroomGroove.com for more advice on everything you ever wanted to know about being a smart groom.

Index